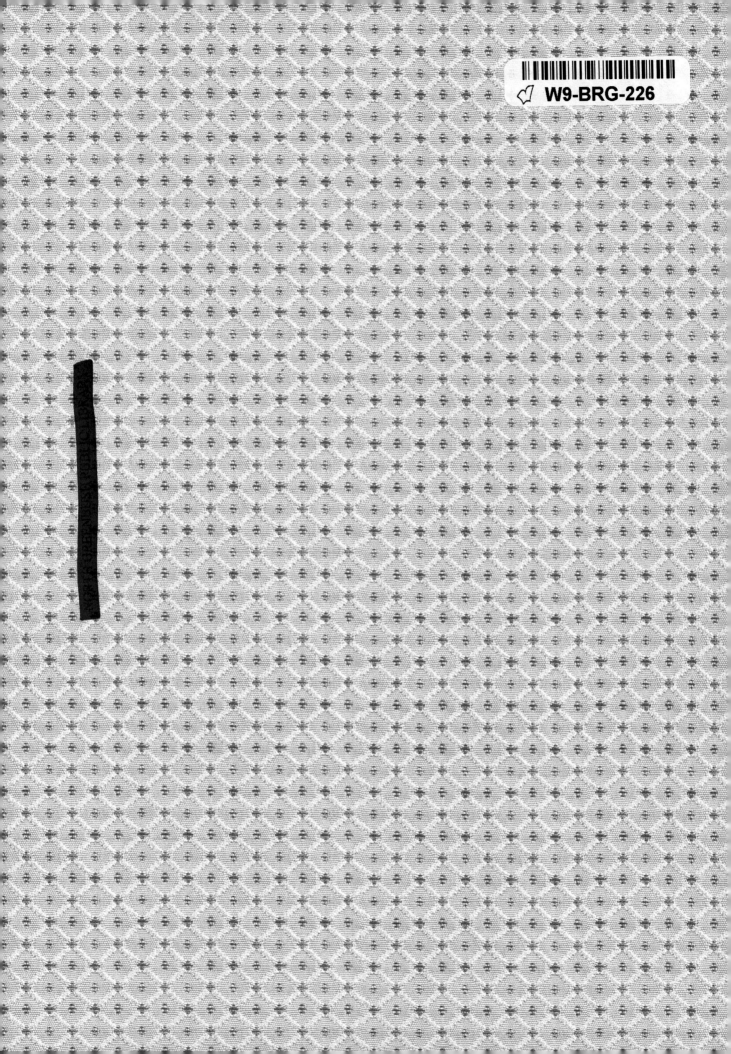

At Home With Laurie Ann

A DECORATOR'S GUIDE:
TURN THE PLACE YOU LIVE INTO A HOME YOU LOVE

LAURIE ANN McMILLIN RAY

LAURIE ANN
PUBLISHING, INC.

Acknowledgements

My heartfelt thanks to Joel Avirom, Jason Snyder and Meghan Day Healey for their talent in designing and creating a beautiful book; David Harrison for his patience and professionalism, which is showcased in his stunning photography; Renee Buchhauser and Jenn Morehead for using their intuitive decorating talent as photo stylists and Cynthia Dial, whose dedication, hard work and expertise made it all happen.

This book is possible because of my friends and family—my husband, children, cousins, aunts, uncles, nieces, nephews, grandparents, brother- and sisters-in-law, brothers and Mom and Dad. Thank you to Erin Dial, the executive manager of my design business, who has been with me from the beginning of this wonderful ride. And a special thanks to everyone who has ever worked for me, worked with me or for whom I have worked.

Photographs © 2009 by David Harrison www.harrisonphotographic.com
Additional photographs © 2009 by Marissa Bouchér, pages 22, 86 (bottom), 121 (top), and 144; and Jim Cox, pages 121 (bottom) and 122–123.

Executive editor: Cynthia Dial
Production by Meghan Day Healey
Book design by Joel Avirom and Jason Snyder

Cataloging-in-Publication Data

Ray, Laurie Ann McMillin.
At home with Laurie Ann : a decorator's guide : turn the place you live into a home you love / Laurie Ann McMillin Ray.
p. cm.
Includes index.
ISBN-13: 978-0-9840748-0-8
ISBN-10: 0-9840748-0-5
1. Interior decoration—United States—History—21st century.   I. Title.
NK2004.15.R39 2010   747'.0973
QBI09-600179

Color separations by Graphic Process Inc.
Printed in USA by Worzalla Publishing

LAURIE ANN PUBLISHING, INC.
P. O. Box 502150
San Diego, CA 92150-2150

To Mom and Dad,
For creating a warm and loving home,
and teaching me to make it matter.

Contents

"*Welcome home*," I'm Laurie Ann McMillin Ray. As a wife, mother, daughter, sister, friend . . . and, yes, a designer, I've never professed that I'm "Martha Stewart," yet home has always been at the heart of my life. It's where I can do positively everything or absolutely nothing.

I wasn't born a designer, but I remember when I became one. At age 15, I was with my mother during a consultation with her interior decorator. We lived in a warm ranch house, the living room was casual and the dilemma was where to position the sofa. The decorator first placed it against the wall, but it wasn't quite right; then in the middle of the room. Still not the best place. I assessed the layout and moved the sofa at an angle. It worked. My simple change pulled the room together and made it instantly inviting. I've been moving furniture since.

My late father, Corky McMillin, was a real estate developer who built 30,000 homes and 16 mixed-use, master-planned communities during the course of his career. It was 1960 when he started his small construction company in Bonita, California, with my mother, Vonnie, who handled the accounting. From the beginning, his philosophy was simple—everyone deserves to own a house.

Like many daughters, I took cues from my father, operating by a similar principle—everyone deserves to make a house his home. I guess that's when my personal doctrine of design (the subject of this book) began.

Shortly after my interior decorating initiation, i.e., my family's living room, my father noticed my potential and in my 20s I began furnishing his model homes. How did this leap from high school football games to high-style floor plans transpire? I looked at the work of his design team and thought, "I can do better than that." And I did.

You may not intuitively see a room's design scheme and think, "I can do better than that." Or even, "I can do that."

But can you turn a house into your home? I say yes. With help, you can. With inspiration, you can. With this book, you can. Now let's get going!

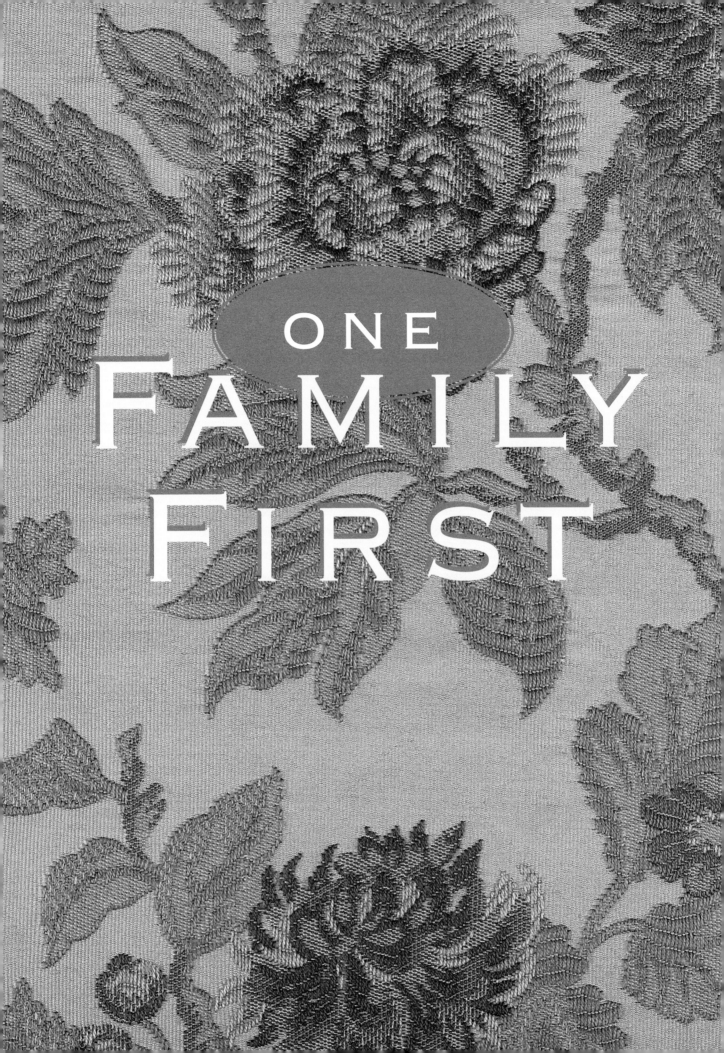

ONE FAMILY FIRST

*F*amily. What does that mean?

It means everything and includes everyone. Throughout my childhood, we spent weekends and holidays with family. My parents were the core of our congregation of kin including my brothers, grandmas, grandpas, aunts, uncles and cousins. Mom and Dad were the role models, known for their honesty, sincerity and loyalty.

I am the only girl between two brothers. My older sibling, Mark, is smart, organized and caring, the quintessential big brother. Scott, the younger one, is a real friend who is as intelligent as he is kind.

For me, growing up was in an Ozzie and Harriet world. As a family, we camped, snow skied, handled four wheelers and drove dune buggies. And during visits to our cabin on the Colorado River, we water skied and rode wave runners. All of those fun and free times reinforced our family unit.

But home was the constant, it was our comfort zone. Mom served everyone-around-the-table family meals and was known for her lavish, yet casual, holiday celebrations. No one wanted to miss a McMillin get-together. And she kept an immaculate house. She considered our organized, comfortable home her gift to us. It was and it is to this day, for Mom is always there and always welcoming.

A weathered wooden sign that greets customers in one of my retail stores best summates my career credo.

Home is where we did it all —

Throughout the book you will find helpful hints in my *Laurie Ann Tip* boxes.

We were taught to make things matter, to treat everything as if it were important. The by-product of our upbringing is that it made me love home. Home is where we did it all—baked cookies, packed lunches, wrapped gifts, chatted over coffee, watched baseball games, solved problems, talked business and supported each other—everything that my family continues to do to this day.

So, now that I'm a wife and a mom of three grown children, Charlotte, Stephanie and Cody, I've repeated my own mother's role, mirroring the life my parents created for my brothers and me.

And I love it!

Annual Christmas parties, impromptu beach barbeques, extended family get-togethers, activities for my husband Rick's profession (Red Hawk Golf Course in Temecula, California) and on-going events for my company—they all fill our calendar.

In turn, I have taken what I learned from my earliest memories of home, embraced it and turned it into an interior design business—a business that is not about style, but about lifestyle.

A weathered wooden sign that greets customers in one of my retail stores best summates my career credo: "Be home, be comfortable, be content. Be you!"

In truth, you *can* go home again.

> WHEN PURCHASING SOMETHING SPECIAL FOR YOURSELF (E.G., PLACEMATS, HOLIDAY DISHES, WINE GLASSES, CANDLEHOLDERS, ETC.), CONSIDER BUYING IN DUPLICATE AS GIFTS FOR RELATIVES. NOT ONLY WILL THEY APPRECIATE YOUR THOUGHTFULNESS, BUT YOU CAN COLLECTIVELY USE THE ITEM(S) FOR LARGE FAMILY GET-TOGETHERS.

FAR LEFT: What a group! Little Brother, Mom, Big Brother and Me.

LEFT: Me and my friend, my hero, my Dad.

TWO

STYLE IN STAGES

"Tall, grande or venti?" inquires a coffee clerk. Interior design is certainly not as easy as ordering a latte, but the similarity goes to the basics. Find a starting point.

Whether you seek an all-out overhaul or a visual shake-up of your home, you'll begin in the same place—with your taste, your needs and your dreams.

SPOT YOUR STYLE

The first step is to determine your style, the vision of your imagination. Sounds easy, doesn't it? But is it?

Consider the opening questions my designers typically ask. "What are your favorite colors to wear?" "What is your fashion style?" Formal? Informal? Or do you know? Personal dress preferences provide clues to the interior design look that will feel most comfortable to you. Think about it. Would you expect someone who prefers casual clothing to enjoy cosmopolitan surroundings? It's unlikely.

Let's continue. Are you simple and sophisticated? Does cozy chic capture your imagination? Would you describe yourself as trendy or traditional? How do you feel about retro? Perhaps you're not exclusively one style or another (many are not), but rather a mix of several of the above. Fret not if you have no ready answers to this impromptu style quiz—help follows.

So keep reading and don't get discouraged. It's easy, I promise.

What are your favorite colors...

STARTING HERE, STARTING NOW

Your assignment is as simple as a trip to the mall.

Visit a bookstore and splurge on an issue of every home, garden, decorating and style magazine that catches your eye. Make it a hobby and take your time. Now sit in a comfy chair with a red marker, a pair of scissors and a large cup of a warm drink.

Flip through the magazines, with one purpose. Find what appeals to you.

When a piece of furniture, a room, a color or a look is to your liking, clip the page from the magazine and make a simple notation with your marker. Your red directives might read: "funky candlesticks," "mixed-pattern chair," perhaps "oversized floral arrangement."

It initially will seem a hodgepodge, but a jumble it is not. It is this research, as informal as it may now seem, that will point to the path of your personal style, the most important tool from this point forward in your design arsenal. Keep in mind that the more time you invest in the project, the more apparent the direction. And take note that during this process *it is important to remember who you are, but don't forget who you want to be.*

Three of my favorite things—
rooster designs, checkered patterns
and the freshness of flowers.

Now, make a file for each room. For example, your outdoor file folder might include garden boxes, barbeque grills, picnic items and more.

Similarities will emerge. You will find you usually select the same colors and prefer the same styles, such as an attraction to green hues or a preference for antique furniture.

Perhaps you'll observe a leaning toward patterns (a specific print style such as floral, stripes or geometric). It may be the simplicity of a neutral wall decorated with a single, dominate painting in primary colors that appeals. Or the boldness of a Swarovski crystal chandelier might catch your eye.

Eventually, your collection of magazine tear-outs will point to an overall personality type of décor or to your own unique style. But you're not finished. As reinforcement, look through books on design and visit decorating stores. It is amazing how external elements stimulate your style, whatever it may be.

And, alas, the inner decorator in you is born.

ANALYZATION

THE HOME OF YOUR IMAGINATION

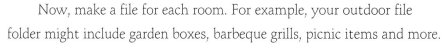

FORMAL

If you lean toward traditional, your decorating style will have few surprises. The symmetry of a perfectly balanced room, the richness of furniture in dark woods, the luxury of silk and velvet fabrics and the appointment of fine antiques capture your look—a timeless one that has transcended generations. In short, things match and they make sense.

ROMANTIC

Haven and home are synonyms for a romantic. Fragrances and lit candles set the mood for a stage replete with floral prints, overflowing window boxes, gauzy curtains and throws tossed over comfy corner chairs. Family is never far—homespun accessories, heirlooms and scattered personal photographs are gentle reminders that if your romantic gene is dominant, home is where the heart is.

TRANQUIL

If comfort and serenity are important perks of your home base, this sanctuary-like style is yours. Earth tone colors, uncluttered room arrangements and warmth encased in simplicity define the look you like. Windows showcasing surrounding nature (perhaps an herb garden) and spa-inspired bathrooms might be on your dream list, but it is orderly calm that most appeals to you. Bottom line: You're not looking for wow factors or over-the-top accents.

CONTEMPORARY

Large, open rooms combined with bold furniture and bare windows help create the sleek and stylish look you seek as a devotee of contemporary design. Signature appointments might include modern art, a leather sofa, marble floors and chrome-and-glass accents. But whatever you chose, the finished product is void of cutesy and clutter.

ECLECTIC

A think-outside-the-box attitude is required to successfully accomplish this look, a compilation of several styles. It is the combination of opposing design elements—furniture from different time periods, unusual color schemes, assorted patterns and distinctive fabrics. To be eclectic, you operate by two informal rules: 1) anything goes (with anything else) and 2) there are no rules.

Think about it—again

Answers to the following questions continue to guide you. They are basic, but enlightening.

1. Who lives in your home? Do any have special needs, e.g., elderly parent unable to climb stairs?

2. Do you have children? What are their ages?

3. Are there pets in your home? How many and what color are they? (Note: A light-colored sofa is a poor choice for a black lap dog.)

4. Is your life in transition? Is your first baby on the horizon? Does your pre-teen want a space to entertain friends? Has your last child left for college? Is retirement around the corner? Is your goal to simplify?

5. What room(s) are you decorating? Who will use the room and for what purpose? Is there an original feature in the space to be considered? Is organization a desired key element? Is lighting (natural or artificial) important? Consider areas such as a library or sewing room and their demand for plentiful light.

6. What atmosphere are you trying to create in the room? Is your end goal a cozy enclave or a hub of activity?

7. Where does your family congregate? Why do they collect there? When do they collect there?

8. What are favorite pastimes, hobbies and home activities of each family member? Which of these activities should be allotted its own space?

9. Do you entertain? Formal sit-down dinners or casual barbeques? Indoors or out of doors? How large are your get-togethers? What seasons do you entertain? (Different times of the year require different considerations.)

STEP BY STEP

MONEY MATTERS—I can work within any budget—many of the principles are the same. However, at the commencement of any design project, the establishment of a spending plan is key—it charts your map's course. Because greater resources do not present the challenges of a smaller bottom line, let's concentrate on the trimmed wallet.

A LESSER BUDGET

- Takes additional time and research to shop around
- Requires greater preparation
- Necessitates purchases that are completely purposeful
- Demands more creativity
- Makes mistakes unaffordable

Initially, these restrictions may seem daunting. But not so. Consider the following solutions, which I have shared over the years with clients and budget-minded, do-it-yourself decorators.

- Check out stores like Target and Pier 1, as well as swap meets and thrift shops. However, don't neglect your city's design center, high-end retailers and decorating boutiques— you may come across a real deal, such as my retail stores (we always have sales).

- There is great value in assessing the importance of every item, and investing accordingly. For example, a game room's largest expenditure should be its chairs, comfortable ones— not the poker table, as the majority of your budget should go to the most useful piece(s) in the room. Rule of thumb: Invest where you sit.

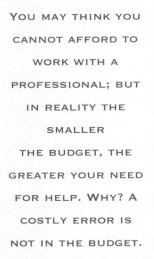

$

YOU MAY THINK YOU CANNOT AFFORD TO WORK WITH A PROFESSIONAL; BUT IN REALITY THE SMALLER THE BUDGET, THE GREATER YOUR NEED FOR HELP. WHY? A COSTLY ERROR IS NOT IN THE BUDGET.

$

HAVE FUN WITH MINOR PURCHASES (THIS IS WHERE YOU CAN MAKE MISTAKES); BUT GET HELP WITH MAJOR BUYS.

$

Design Services AVAILABLE

- Think about adding accents, rather than making major changes. Keep in mind that small details can have significant impact, e.g., changing out door knobs, adding molding and painting kitchen cabinets. Let your creativity shine, as we did by adding a painted plaid design to kitchen cabinet doors in colors that enhanced both the room's window coverings and its distinctive tile backsplash.

- Mix high-end with low-end—splurge on a good couch and arrange it with favorite, but less expensive older pieces.

- Seek frugal finds—purchase floor model furniture (at discounts), sift through fabric clearance bins for expensive remnants to be used for smaller items (example: pillows) and visit consignment stores in wealthy areas (e.g., La Jolla, Beverly Hills and Aspen), great sources for top-end furniture and accessories at a fraction of their original price tags.

ASSESS THE ARCHITECTURE—Are you working with a narrow, compact room that requires creative organization? Maybe your family room is so large, clusters of individual seating areas are necessary to instill a sense of home. Do your bedroom's floor-to-ceiling windows beg to frame the view?

DETERMINE THE MOST IMPORTANT ITEM(S)—This can be a tricky task, because it may take a trained eye to recognize your room's most significant visual. I have worked with many clients who are blind when it comes to their own homes' potential—it could be the brick floors, the French doors hidden behind heavy drapes or the kitchen's green tile from the 1950s. Once you've made the determination, showcase it—make it standout!

OVERLEAF: Take advantage of your home's architecture and frame your view.

WORK WITH WHAT YOU HAVE—The feel, the look, the theme—concentrate on what you have, *not what you don't have*. Start with something important—with what emotionally charges or drains you, perhaps where you spend the most time. Positives usually outweigh the negatives and help you emphasize the best features of a room.

That said, if the task at hand is a negative—fix it, update it and remember that sometimes it just needs to be fluffed. Let's say you hate your bedspread, couch, or kitchen—then that's where you begin.

FAMILY-TIZE IT—Your house is about those who live there—it should fit your family. To accomplish this task, get family members involved because their opinions matter. If you have three kids and five dogs, it is not the time in your life for white couches—those will come later. And don't neglect to create your family's favorite place. My family's spot is our kitchen. Because it's where we hang out, I even have a sofa in the room.

IDENTIFY THEMES—A theme can be a pink-and-white princess room for your daughter or an Americana-style study for a patriotic family member. It can be generated by your desire to turn your small home into a warm, cabin-like getaway or to create an island-inspired beach retreat. If you're a collector, you have themes. But beware—for at risk is the tendency to go overboard, to create more of a Disneyland-like amusement park than a tasteful, comfortable home.

SELECT A COLOR—Assess the feel, the look and the theme when choosing a paint color. Additionally, take into account your geographical location, climate and the style of your home. Your selection could be simply because you love the color (refer to your quiz revelations), perhaps you want to match a color from the room's painted buffet (your grandmother's treasured antique) or maybe you're going with a specific motif (e.g., blue and red in keeping with the nautical look for your son, an avid sailor).

...don't neglect to create your family's favorite place.

If you're a collector, you have themes.

Your color choice could be pre-destined. Let's say your vintage bathroom tile is Wedgewood in color—the obvious selection is one that complements this shade of blue. However, keep in mind that if the tile is old and the color seems outdated, you can bring the room into the 21st century by introducing a current color combination (such as chocolate brown and turquoise blue), whether it's with paint, rugs or towels.

SWATCH IT!—Act like a designer and create a sample board—paint chips, alongside fabric, wallpaper and carpet swatches. (Tip: It can be as simple as using an 8½ x 11-inch piece of paper.) Are the elements complementary to one another or do they appear disjointed? Try different combinations until you get it right, and take note. Observe your selections in all possible light conditions within the room you are decorating—under artificial lighting and by natural light (from bright sunshine to cloud covered days).

LAY ASIDE THE LAYOUT—Remove all the furniture, window coverings, the entire contents from the space you are decorating. Wipe from your memory where everything was, what it looked like. Designate your *anchor* (your focal point). It is the room's most important item; it is always something you love. Place it in the room and continue, adding furniture—piece by piece—where you want it and where it works. Adapt to traffic patterns; create paths within the room for people to pass through.

Remember, there is no obligation to use everything—get rid of what you don't use or no longer like (or paint it). Nor is there an obligation to use only pieces exclusive to that room—pull from the entire house to fill the holes. You can make any room new with old furnishings from another area of your home.

However, be mindful that as important as the space you fill is the space you leave empty.

Try different combinations until you get it right...

ELEMENTS OF DESIGN

Decorating is all about the successful combination of the room's five basic features—walls, floors, furniture, window coverings and lighting. But don't forget that during this process the application of the basic fundamentals of scale, proportion, harmony and balance is always important.

1. **WALLS**—These four vertical surfaces are akin to the setting of a stage play, for they are the backdrop of the entire room. Think about it. The very size of a room's walls (compared to the other elements) makes them significant. Two directions are possible: walls can inconspicuously blend with the room's additional components or make a statement—standing on their own. Through walls you achieve the atmosphere of a room, whether it is warm, sunny, cool or cozy. In short, you set the atmosphere you want.

Though there is a variation of wallcoverings—from fabric and tile, to paneling and mirrors—your two basic choices are paint and wallpaper.

IF A PAINT STORE DOESN'T OFFER THE EXACT SHADE OF PAINT YOU SEEK, VISIT WITH A SAMPLE OF THE CARPET, WALLPAPER, FABRIC, WHATEVER YOU WANT TO MATCH, AND HAVE A CUSTOM COLOR BLENDED. IT WILL COST MORE, BUT IT WILL BE WORTH IT.

PAINT—Should you select paint, decisions don't end here. After picking the color, a finish must be selected—flat, satin, gloss or semi-gloss. And if going beyond a solid color painted wall, you have creative options—among them are sponging, striping, washing, texturing, stenciling and trompe l'oeil painting.

OPPOSITE: After picking a color, a finish must be selected.

OVERLEAF: Set the mood of the room with color.

$

BUY ONE ROLL
OF YOUR CHOICE
OF WALLPAPER
AND TAPE SEVERAL
FLOOR-TO-CEILING
STRIPS OF THE
PAPER ONTO THE
"POTENTIAL"
WALL TO GAUGE
ITS LONG-TERM
APPEAL.

$

WALLPAPER—This wall covering option is expansive. From florals and stripes to checks and plaids, a popular selection is patterned wallpaper—large-scale and small-scale—making proper proportion to the room's size a consideration. Other choices include grass weaves, faux-cork, metallics, rice paper, murals and simple borders. Wallpaper can also be a less expensive imitation of a natural element along the lines of wood, stone or bamboo. And it can create the illusion of fabrics, such as silk and suede.

DON'T BE AFRAID TO GO WITH BEADBOARDING. IT'S ONE OF MY FAVORITE WAYS TO ENHANCE THE LOOK OF A WALL.

2. **FLOORS**—Your best flooring choice depends on your family—who it consists of and how they use your home. Because flooring takes the bulk of your home's wear (but can be neglected when it comes to care), obvious considerations are durability (lifespan) and maintenance. But don't forget these additional, but equally important factors: comfort and its statement of style.

Considering the many options—from stone, wood and ceramic to vinyl sheeting, wall-to-wall carpeting and area rugs—you might be floored by the possibilities. There is no right or wrong, just floor facts.

HERE ARE A FEW (OF MANY)

- VINYL FLOORING is stain-resistant, easy to maintain and can be a less expensive choice. It's a great selection for a family with kids and dogs. And today's brick and flagstone patterns look as authentic as the real thing.

- CARPET creates cozy, and it absorbs sound.

- The look of a NATURAL WOOD floor is rich and luxuriant.

- TILE caters to high-traffic areas, as well as kitchens and bathrooms. A consideration is that it can be a difficult surface to stand on for lengthy periods, making the use of a kitchen rug a practical decision. Note: While handmade ceramic tile is decorative and durable, it is costly.

- New on the scene are FASHION-FORWARD TILES . . . they include contemporary op art or bold graphic patterns, even wood and metal look-alikes.

- Floor design, such as a glazed TILE PATTERN, must be in harmony with your other design elements.

- AREA RUGS define small, intimate zones within a larger space. A creative area rug will become your room's anchor. And while a rug may create a theme and add color, it can be easily replaced when trends change.

- Tipping the price scale is a floor of NATURAL STONE (e.g., marble, tumbled marble, granite and slate).

Confused? Don't be. My advice: Identify your family's needs,
do the homework, weigh the facts and go for it.

3. **FURNITURE**—At first glance, furniture selection can be overwhelming. Among the many considerations are type, style, price, dimensions (its scale to the room and other pieces of furniture), manufacturer and materials (e.g., upholstered, wrought iron, rattan, wicker, natural woods, among others).

But intimidating it is not if you are mindful of the three furniture fundamentals: personal style, price and purpose.

PERSONAL STYLE—After the earlier assignment and quiz, your own style should be established (and, if not, hopefully emerging). Once you're headed in a design direction, adhere to this rule—the style of furniture should work with your décor. And avoid trend.

PRICE—Your investment is pre-determined by your budget, though the most costly couch is not necessarily your wisest selection—nor is the cheapest. This is where your comparative shopping skills, coupled with a solid understanding of your needs, translate to good value (regardless of the number of 0's you are able, or unable, to write on the check). Don't overanalyze. Buy the best you can afford, and keep in mind that some furniture is not forever.

PURPOSE—The intention of any piece of furniture is established by the "s" factor. Do you sit upon it? Is it for sleeping? Will you have supper atop it? Or will you use it for storage?

Next, weigh the importance of its purpose in your lifestyle. If you are an avid entertainer, invest in a showcase dining room. Conversely, if your children are young and weekends are centered around your time together, get a great farm table for dining and spend your money on a comfortable, durable family room.

SELECT FURNITURE WITH PERSONALITY TO MAKE A STATEMENT OF YOUR STYLE.

FURNITURE
SELECTION

Final step. Factor in the possibility of double-duty furnishings (example: a guest's hide-a-bed doubling as a sitting room couch) and the unexpected-use furniture piece (e.g., an intricately carved wooden dining table used as an office desk).

In my own home, I've turned a small space into a nurturing nook. It's cozy enough for coffee and comfy enough to spend the day curled up with a best-selling book. And I've followed my own decorating advice—tucking an old drop-leaf table behind the love seat to hold a large vase of flowers until it's needed as a tabletop for an intimate meal or afternoon tea.

FURNITURE SETS
ARE PASSÉ.
NO LONGER IS A
FULLY-MATCHED
BEDROOM OR
LIVING ROOM
ENSEMBLE
STYLISH.
AND IT'S LESS
FUN THAN
COMBINING
PIECES
USING YOUR
IMAGINATION
AS A GUIDE.

WINDOW
COVERINGS

4. WINDOW COVERINGS—To me, window coverings are like the chips in a chocolate chip cookie. They are so essential an ingredient, a room is incomplete without them. Their purpose is simple—to frame a window from both the inside-out and the outside-in. They additionally control the light, give you privacy, highlight a view or set a state of mind. Window coverings cozy up any space.

Statements are made by both style and fabric. While swags and draperies say formal, pleated shades, Venetian blinds and shutters produce a clean silhouette. Even the length of the drapes impacts the appearance. For a tidy, casual look, hang drapes so that they just touch the floor; but for a grander flair, let the fabric luxuriously pool atop it. Fabric choice tells an additional tale. Voile is light and airy, silk is elegant, linen is crisp, velvet is luscious, calico is country and the list goes on.

Not to be overlooked is hardware, typically the final touch. Your window treatments are fine-tuned by details such as decorative rods, finials and holdbacks, as well as tassels and fabric tiebacks. Example: To add a dramatic dash to an ordinary window, secure each side of your open curtains with brackets, but place them higher than usual.

And window coverings can mask countless architectural flaws. For a window that is too small, raise a shade or a valance above the opening so that it appears taller. When dealing with multiple, but different sized windows, create the impression of similarity with curtains of the same dimension.

> FOR A SUBTLE TRANSFORMATION OF A ROOM, CONSIDER LINING YOUR CURTAINS IN A COLOR (OPPOSED TO WHITE OR OFF-WHITE). BUT WHATEVER COLOR YOU SELECT, KEEP IT CONSISTENT—WHEN VIEWING FROM OUTSIDE THE HOUSE, THE LOOK SHOULD BE THE SAME.

5. LIGHTING—The facts are simple. Lighting guides a room's mood (as well as the mood of those in the room).

In the past, you may have relegated the lighting component to secondary status. Like an afterthought, it wasn't until the room was painted, the window coverings were in place, the area rugs positioned and the furniture arranged that you addressed lighting.

Am I correct? Well, no more.

The job to find the right lights for all areas of your home is a big one, but by no means is it an impossible assignment. Let's begin.

A good start is to determine three things: 1) where you want the lighting, 2) when you need the lighting and 3) what style of lighting

LET THERE
BE LIGHT

fixture reflects your décor. And keep in mind that natural lighting is always a gift if you effectively manage it. It gives the house a glow and gives you more options because colors appear true.

CONTINUE . . .

DETERMINE how much lighting you desire by establishing its purpose: task or ambient.

OPERATE by the principle, *a little goes a long way*, and apply accordingly. Use a singular spot light to dramatically accent artwork or set a serene scene with candlelight.

EXPLORE how your lighting options affect a room's color.

THINK beyond the illumination value to its decorative merit. Example: Use a table or floor lamp to introduce a theme (e.g., a pear-adorned table lamp in your kitchen).

SHY AWAY from a bright, overhead fixture to fill the room's every need. Tip: Use dimmer bulbs and switches with assorted lamps.

UNDERSTAND that the bigger the chandelier, the greater the impact. This style of lighting fixture makes a significant focal point in any room.

FOR A REASONABLE, fun and more up-to-date way to light a room, consider track lighting. With today's selections, no longer are they the unimaginative eyesores of the past.

DECORATE WITH MIRRORS. NOT ONLY DO THEY GIVE THE ILLUSION OF LARGER SPACE, BUT ADDITIONALLY AMPLIFY YOUR ROOM'S LIGHT SOURCES (BOTH EXTERIOR AND INTERIOR).

OPPOSITE:
Use a table or floor lamp to introduce a theme.

My Style, My Way

My style wasn't taught in the classroom, it was learned at home. Of course, home is defined differently by anyone you would ask. But to me, it is distressed or unfinished furniture mixed with overstuffed upholstered chairs and sofas you melt into, a blend of patterned fabrics, scattered armoires topped with family knickknacks and greenery, collections of heirlooms, high-end antiques and yard-sale treasures.

Dishes my mother purchased for me in Europe line my dining room's china cabinet, wicker baskets display fresh produce on my kitchen counter and pieces from my collection of ceramic roosters are selectively scattered everywhere.

Currently, my favorite color combination is apple green and chocolate brown. But these preferences change—as should yours—there's no need to be stagnant.

My home is a reflection of my motto—mix and don't match. I believe in shaking it up. Make it yours, and you will always love coming home and being home!

OVERLEAF: My home is a reflection of my family.

IF YOU FIND YOURSELF OVERWHELMED WITH DESIGN DILEMMAS, USE THE SERVICES OF AN INTERIOR DECORATOR, IF ONLY FOR ANAHOUR OR SO OF CONSULTATION TIME. BUT MAKE SURE THE RESULTS FOLLOW YOUR TASTE, NOT THE DESIGNER'S— IT'S YOUR HOME.

THREE
ROOM BY ROOM

$\mathcal{E}$very room is distinctive—with a different purpose, for different people and with different considerations, some being substantial challenges. When in decorating mode, there is no need to tackle the entire house simultaneously. But whether you address the rooms one by one, or every other one, pay attention to their collective compatibility.

One way to tie all areas of your home together is through color. Design your rooms to borrow colors from one another. How so? In each room consider using occasional furniture pieces of the same color (perhaps casual white or elegant black). Or think about painting the baseboards and doors in your entry, halls and common areas the same color. Either of these examples will help walk the eye from one room to the next and will create an illusion of flowing space.

Remember, rooms establish boundaries: Mom and Dad's space, the place to work, your eating area and so on. The key to room-by-room success is to understand their differences. Let's explore them.

OPPOSITE: Pay attention to your rooms' collective compatibility.

RIGHT: Design your rooms to borrow colors from one another—this style creates an illusion of flowing space.

ENTRY

Don't Hesitate, Decorate

"How many first impressions do you get?" is a question I ask clients when illustrating the importance of their entry. In terms of square footage, the area may be small; but if you are talking impact, its significance is sizable. The proper purpose of your entry is to provide a peek of the interior beyond. It's a glimpse and a tease of what's coming.

Where does this preview begin? With your front door—both exterior and interior. Your door should say "welcome," a greeting that extends through your entry. Don't try to make it too functional. An opportunity is missed if you don't treat this nook as an enclave of décor. Your back hall is the area for practical details, such as hooks for coats, racks for boots and shelves for mail.

The task of decorating your entry does not have to be an expensive one. The area is a custom-made space to display family photos, showcase collections or accent with a mirror. A larger entry gives more latitude. Its furnishing possibilities include chairs, ottomans, side tables or small desks, enhanced by rugs. The goal in my own home was to create an entry comfortable enough to want to linger; consequently, it's an area where we sometimes gather.

CONSIDERATIONS

- Make your entry warm, welcoming and wow!

- Choose a funky color for your front door—it will take your look to the next level.

- Take into account weather conditions when selecting flooring (e.g., tile floors for rainy days or snowy winters; wooden floors to give a sense of warmth).

- Set the mood of your home with your entry's lighting; it can range from well-lit and functional to a romantic, low-light level statement.

- Decorate at eye level in a small entry. Because of its size, it will be a portion of the house where guests seldom idle.

LIVING ROOM

The importance of your living room goes beyond its expected functions—entertaining and gathering. More than any area of your home, the style of the entire house is set by the look of the living room. It's like the first act of a play.

So make it matter—make it cozy and comfortable. If you don't use your living room, make it a room you will use.

If your home has a family room, you can design a more formal living room. But regardless of how beautifully it is decorated, your living room should be functional. Create a favorite place to talk on the telephone. Establish a quiet getaway—a place to visit (a rare luxury today)—it's where my mother and I always retreat to when she comes to see me.

My unbreakable rule is to follow this logic: Make your living room livable.

CONSIDERATIONS

- Create a room of beauty—one enhanced with lamps, floral arrangements, pictures and lit candles.

- Give the room a purpose (e.g., set up a table with a complicated jigsaw puzzle in this out-of-the-way haven).

- Group furniture into smaller sitting areas for added interest and intimacy (if space allows).

- Select a strong visual anchor—a fireplace, favorite artwork or one-of-a-kind furniture piece (something personal and special that reflects your taste).

OPPOSITE: Think about changing accents and room details with the change of the seasons.

OVERLEAF: More than any area of your home, the style of the entire house is set by the look of the living room.

DINING ROOM

If the dining room is where your family usually eats, practicality is your guide. But if this room is used only for entertaining and special occasions, get ready to make a statement. This is where your creative juices can concentrate.

Establish an environment in sync with its purpose. Is it a room where you hang out, visit with guests, relax with family? Determine its objective and design toward that goal.

A thoughtfully appointed dining room can both showcase your style and signal the importance you place on sharing meals with family and friends. Your fabric choices and the style of your table and chairs establish an atmosphere—whether it's cheery, sophisticated, funky or casual.

CONSIDERATIONS

- Decorate around something exceptional—the table's centerpiece, your antique hutch, a spectacular chandelier or a bold area rug beneath the table.

- Remember that the dimensions of your dining table should be the largest that the room will accommodate—allowing adequate space between the table and the wall—for ease of getting in and out of the chairs. A fun variation might be two smaller round tables.

- Select a rug that permits easy chair maneuverability and is sized to an expanded table (when all the leaves and extra chairs are used).

Decorate around something exceptional...

OPPOSITE: Your choice of table and chairs establishes an atmosphere.

OVERLEAF: A thoughtfully appointed dining room can showcase your style.

Nothing creates

FAMILY ROOM

Like its name, *family room*, this space is for every member of your household—each using the area in his or her own way (many times concurrently). Though only a partial list, family room activities can include entertaining, watching television and movies, playing games, listening to music, reading books, using the computer, pursuing hobbies, awaiting meal time and just plain lounging.

Sound like a challenge to design one room to adapt to all of the above? It can be, but not for you if you follow these directives.

Design a gathering spot where it's easy to relax (even in fabric selections) and with comfortable seating, inviting smells, snug throw blankets and an alluring fireplace. Because the fireplace is invariably the anchor of any room, showcase it (e.g., decorate the mantel, use a distinctive fire screen, top it with artwork or a family photo). Nothing creates a magnet for gathering like the warmth of a fire. Use stools and benches to seat everyone where they want to be. Remember: This room is all about being together, being cozy and being relaxed.

Don't forget: It must also be practical. So, look for flexible furniture pieces—ones that conform to the situation—a modular sofa that can be reconfigured in minutes, an ottoman that transforms into a tabletop and movable pieces such as stools and occasional chairs. And have fun with whimsical inclusions like an antique birdcage.

If working with a great room (one big room containing your family room and kitchen), coordinate but differentiate each zone. Create an invisible line of demarcation. You can distinguish the family area from your kitchen space by painting your television wall unit

a magnet for gathering like the warmth of a fire—

OPPOSITE: The fireplace is invariably the anchor of any room, showcase it (e.g., decorate the mantel, use a distinctive fire screen, top it with artwork or a family photo).

differently than your kitchen cabinetry. And you can make the space appear longer by selecting related (not exactly matching) rugs in both areas.

The family room is the place to showcase *you*—display your needlepoint pillow, the children's artwork, your husband's photography. Design it so that even if visitors don't know you, the family room will tell them about you.

CONSIDERATIONS

- Avoid solid, light colors in this busy room. Fashion it for function—lying on the couch, eating snacks, drinking pop and watching television. If you have kids, create a room you aren't afraid for them to use.

- Design for storage. Eliminate the look of clutter—place televisions, sound systems and DVDs behind closed doors; have rattan baskets to hold throws and small bins to organize your children's toys or house your favorite magazines.

- Make certain your television screen provides a good view from every angle. Choose window treatments that open and close easily and eliminate the glare of sunlight . . . for television and movie watching. To optimize surround-sound, center your seating between the speakers.

KITCHEN

This room is the center of your home! It's where you cook chili for ball games, make lunches for school and serve pizza snacks to your kids' friends. It all happens in the kitchen.

But though it is the undisputed heart of your home, your kitchen is about more than love. It's about a multi-functional space that is the epicenter for food preparation, meal clean-up, eating and just hanging out.

If the room is a visual extension of other rooms, coordinate it with those rooms—it's crucial; if not, this is an area where your style can deviate.

Let's start at its natural inception—kitchen cabinet choice. Whatever the style, from well-worn scrubby to rich cherry wood, your selection establishes the lines and flow of the room.

Next step: Pick your countertops. Don't worry about what's popular, because today's top counter rule is to follow your taste—whether it is marble, granite, limestone, concrete, stainless steel, tile or wood. Sometimes the counter sets the mood for the kitchen

The sleek look of stainless appliances works with any style; it's very popular and great for re-sale. And if you go with color, all appliances should be the same—for continuity.

FOR ADDED FLAIR, REMOVE SEVERAL CABINET DOORS. USE GLASS PANEL DOORS OR CHICKEN WIRE IN PLACE OF GLASS TO SHOWCASE SHELVES DISPLAYING COLORFUL COOKWARE.

OPPOSITE AND RIGHT: If your kitchen is a visual extension of other rooms, coordinate it with those rooms—it's crucial; if not, this is an area where your style can deviate.

Lastly, your kitchen table should say, "Come in and sit down." Table style is very important. Follow the basic rules of design and choose one that blends with the rest of the room and one that fits your lifestyle (e.g., an oversized pine table for an active family versus a shiny metal selection for the single urbanite).

CONSIDERATIONS

- Be gutsy—get creative with your kitchen counter selection (e.g., bright color, chunky stone or sleek and streamlined). And carry that creativity to your tile backsplash.

- Think about the benefits of a round kitchen table—it makes it possible for everyone to look at one another and visit when dining.

- Don't forget your guests and size the table to allow for additional diners (decorate your home with extra chairs, scattering them throughout the house so that they can be added to the table at any given time).

- Use the room to display kitchen-esque collections, such as copper kettles, vintage cooking gadgets and distinctive teapots (my own teapot collection is showcased in a giant hutch in our kitchen).

USE YOUR KITCHEN SPACE FOR THE FAMILY MESSAGE CENTER—DECORATE WITH A HUGE CLOCK AND AN OVERSIZED CHALK BOARD (USING DIFFERENT CHALK COLORS FOR INDIVIDUAL FAMILY MEMBER'S PHONE CALLS, REMINDERS, ETC.).

ABOVE AND OPPOSITE:
Be creative with your tile backsplash.

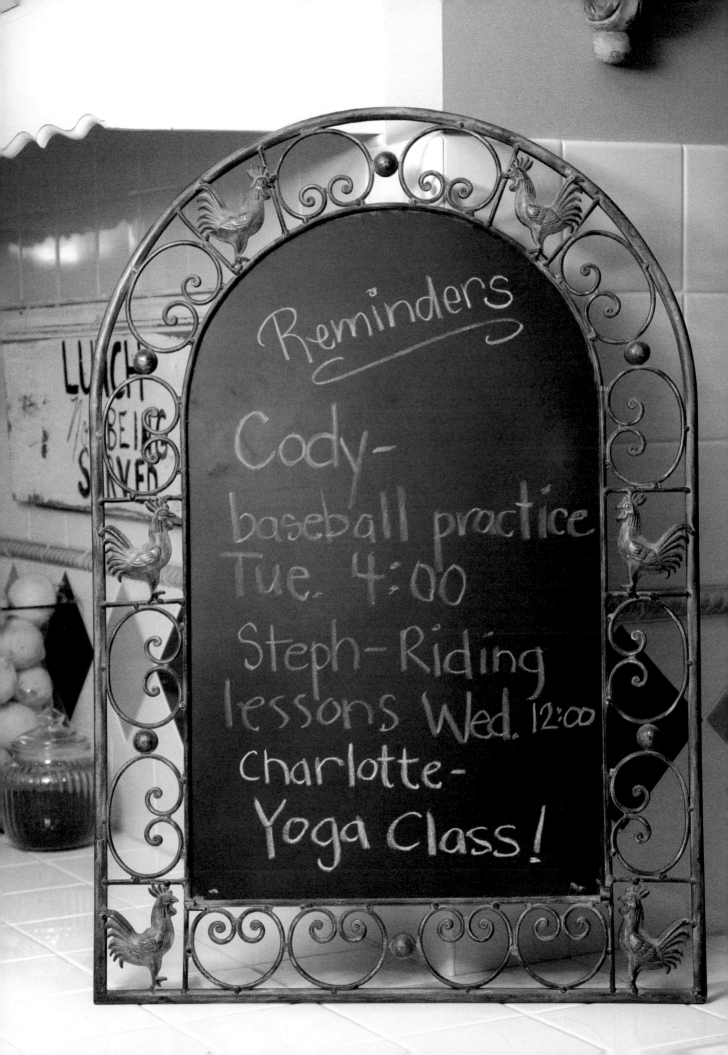

MASTER BEDROOM

Make this room your sanctuary—where you can close the door on the world. Your bedroom's functions are actually primal—sleep, relaxation and rejuvenation.

When it comes to your bedroom, remember that if it makes you cozy and comfortable, it works.

Personalize it—make it yours, his or hers. If you're married, your task is to create a room conducive to your alone couple time.

You have a little levity when it comes to master bedroom color choices, which can be a variation of those used in the rest of your home or your favorite color. The decision is important, for it is this choice that creates the room's feel. For example, a bedroom in monochromatic colors (the shades, tints and tones of one color) replicates the type of room you might find in a multi-star resort. Or think outside the box and consider a bold color—it's very dramatic.

Decorate around the premise that an irresistible bedroom begins with an irresistible bed. Your bed is the room's centerpiece—its bed frame establishes the look of the room. Along these lines, your choices are many: iron bed, platform bed, four-poster canopy bed and sleigh bed, among others. Go beyond the expected and in place of a headboard,

> **FOR A CUSTOM TOUCH, UPHOLSTER YOUR HEADBOARD AND THE BED'S BOX SPRING, ELIMINATING THE NEED FOR A BED SKIRT.**

hang an intricate tapestry, a silk kimono, a colorful patchwork quilt or a weathered door, old gate or fence behind the bed.

But everything should not only look good, it must feel good.

CONSIDERATIONS

- Contemplate the value of lighting for tasks, such as reading in bed (swing-arm lamps on each side of the bed). And don't neglect staging the mood with light: Use candles and set dimmers on fixtures.

- Spend money on the following must-haves: full-length mirror, light-blocking window treatments and adequate storage—his-and-her dressers (for clothing) and nightstands (to accommodate incidentals).

- If you can splurge, think about these items: a coffee maker, bench at the foot of the bed (to sit upon when dressing), lounge chair (next to a side table with a lamp) and a music system (Bose is my choice because it's contained in a portable SoundDock).

Never underestimate the importance of investing in a top-of-the-line mattress and premium bed linens. The texture, color, design and the way you layer linens create an impression (e.g., animal-print says fun, whereas lace and frills spell romance).

Tried-and-true tip: Start with the best of basics (a minimum 400 thread-count bed sheet set), add equally comfortable components and layer luxuriously. Why the fuss? The purpose of all of the above is to provide a good night's rest. What could be more important to your well being?

LAT

Don't be stymied by traditional, off-the-shelf bedding ensembles. Mix in your grandmother's antique linens, flea market finds and assorted patterns. Layer your bed with quilts, throws and decorative pillows. And change your bedding with the season.

CHILDREN'S ROOM

Before decorating this room, consult your client—your child. Determine what is important to him, and within limits, design around this input.

Themes are always popular—their interests, hobbies, make-believe (e.g. puppets, baseball, fairies). But keep in mind that while themes appeal to children of all ages, these motifs change as they get older. No worries: Theme transformation is as easy as a fresh coat of paint and different accessories.

Regardless of age, your goal is to create a pleasant, sturdy and safe refuge for your child, designed to make him want to retreat to his room—not yours. Make it age appropriate. To do so, work from a list of expected activities.

Here are the facts. An infant's primary use of the area is to sleep (though even at this age, the room's predominant purpose is to stimulate the baby's interest). Toddlers use their rooms for sleeping and playing. When your child begins school, the room's action expands from sleeping and being with friends to doing home-

CONSIDER DESK
LIGHTS AND LAMPS
ON THE BED STAND
FOR TASK LIGHT-
ING; BUT AVOID
FLOOR LAMPS—A
POOR MATCH FOR
AN ACTIVE CHILD.

work. Appeal to your teen's desire for independence, but keep it simple and easy to manage.

Remember: Every child should have personal space for his individual needs and storage to accommodate those needs (bookshelves, bins, desks and perhaps customized closet systems).

And always select fabrics for durability and fun. After all, you're only young once!

CONSIDERATIONS

- Devise an orderly environment. Rotate toys. Make floor space for play by placing furniture against the walls, following the informal rule that while walls can be cluttered, clutter should be kept off the floor.

- Design the room so that it's easy to clean up. For storage, note that heavy lids on containers can be dangerous and difficult for children to handle. And shy away from an oversized trunk where seeking one small toy can mean emptying its entire contents.

- Use colored baskets. They'll help you organize without being too rigid.

- Think originality—paint the room your child's favorite color, sketch clouds on the ceiling or illustrate a scene from their favorite children's story with a custom wall mural.

- Take the door off a closet, hang a curtain and transform the space into a playhouse.

IN PLACE OF CLOSETS, USE
BRIGHTLY-COLORED METAL
SCHOOL-LIKE LOCKERS FOR
CLOTHING. COMPLEMENT THE
LOOK WITH METAL FILING
CABINETS (PAINTED THE SAME
HIGH-GLOSS COLOR) FOR
ADDITIONAL STORAGE. OR GO
WITH ONE OF MY FAVORITES,
AN ARMOIRE. IT WILL PROVIDE
AMPLE SPACE AND MAKE THE
CHORE OF CLEAN-UP EASY.
SHOVE IT IN AND CLOSE
THE DOOR!

GUEST ROOM

Greet your guests with a room that is welcoming and comfortable. How do you do this? Do not furnish with leftovers and never use old bedding. Create space for their clothing (closet and drawer space); and if possible, designate an entire dresser as theirs.

Décor should be light, airy and inviting. Colors can be soft ones or crisp white—tones that make you feel like you're on vacation. And keep in mind that while white furniture is like a blank canvas, scrubby furniture gives a homespun flair.

My personal touch is to overload my guest room with comfort items—bottled water, an alarm clock, toiletries, suntan lotion, books, a local map, perhaps a disposable camera. Add a vase of your visitor's favorite flowers, preferred magazines, a framed photo of someone they love and a luxurious terry cloth robe hung on a decorative hook—your houseguest will be at home.

FOR AN EASY TRANSITION FROM A LITTLE GIRL'S TO A YOUNG WOMAN'S ROOM (AND THE EVENTUAL TRANSFORMATION TO A GUEST ROOM), THINK IN TERMS OF SOFT COLORS, CLASSIC FURNITURE AND ANTIQUE ACCENTS.

CONSIDERATIONS

- Place a rattan trunk at the foot of the bed supplied with fresh towels, pillows and extra blankets.

- Treat your visitor to a whimsical surprise—place a yellow rubber duck on the side of your guest bathtub—just for fun!

BATHROOM

Furnish this room as an at-home spa. Load it with candles (smells are important), bath salts, facial products, lotions, fluffy towels, a magnified mirror and lighting for task (and mood). Your bathroom should be as posh as any other room of your house.

A second bathroom for other family members is deemed essential in today's modern world. And in larger households, a powder room can showcase an anything-goes décor. This is where you can use dramatic colors for pizzazz!

Though the general rule of thumb is that the bathroom's color scheme should be compatible with its adjoining room (e.g., the master bedroom, the hall or the foyer), the look of a powder room has greater latitude.

White is never wrong for a bathroom—its translation is clean and crisp. It sets a neutral backdrop for accessories. Color accents can be added with tile trim, towels, shower curtains, rugs, even specialty soaps. And if you paint your walls a color, complement the room with white towels (accented with color).

> DECORATE OUT OF THE NORM. LINE THE WALL NEXT TO A FREESTANDING TUB WITH BOOKSHELVES, MAKING YOUR DREAM OF DEVOURING A GOOD BOOK IN A HOT BATH YOUR EVERYDAY REALITY.

CONSIDERATIONS

- If it's not built-in, create your own storage (e.g., large willow baskets for rolled bath towels or a small scrubbed dresser for grooming essentials). Fill sterling silver topped glass bottles with face lotions, cleansers, etc.

- Use indoor/outdoor fabric to withstand a wet, humid atmosphere; and fill empty spots with moisture loving plants.

- Add a small corner chair with a cute slipcover (for sitting while applying fresh polish to toenails).

- Select a sink that is a piece of furniture (e.g., a pedestal sink or console sink).

BATHROOMS SELDOM
HAVE FOCAL POINTS.
CREATE YOUR OWN WITH
A CLAWFOOT BATHTUB, AN
UNEXPECTED CHANDELIER
OR AN ORNATE, OVERSIZED
MIRROR BESIDE THE TUB
(ADDITIONAL BONUS:
IT VISUALLY OPENS
THE ROOM).

OFFICE

Whether you work at home or take work home, operate by the premise that clutter equals chaos when designing this room. Though the space should be visually pleasing, it also must integrate technology with your needs. The bottom line is clear. For a piece to be an effective office component, it's not enough to simply look good. It should be functional and stylish—they are not mutually exclusive.

The key is organization. An ideal workspace is customized. Start with your anchor—a desk (size matters; it must fit within your space, but accommodate your needs)—maybe an old desk modified with hidden portals. Add comfortable seating. Accent with prints, cover a wall with a bookshelf and finish with task lighting. Don't forget your coffee warmer. *Voilà* . . . you have an office.

CONSIDERATIONS

■ Incorporate eye-pleasing organizational tools as wall decorations—oversized calendars, whiteboards and corkboards, perhaps a large linen pinboard for notes and photos.

■ Place your desktop within the confines of an armoire or a closet to maximize a small area and conceal your workspace, allowing you to simply shut the door at day's end.

TOP LEFT: Think about adding accents.

LEFT: Organize with color.

OPPOSITE: Assess the architecture.

GETAWAY ROOM

What does getaway mean to you? It could be a hobby room, game room, movie room, maybe a porch with a hammock. Or you can have a room "just because"—that is the purpose.

Make it practical—do not design a shrine that will go unused. If you want a perfect getaway room, make it a perfect but make it usable.

You probably don't have enough rooms in your house for all of your family's interests. Most don't. If this is the case, create a multi-function room. An example is a game room where the table can be used for a Scrabble match and double as a gift wrapping station, as easily as it can be covered with plywood and a large tablecloth when serving a buffet.

Even if you don't have the space for a getaway room, create a special corner in your home with an inviting chair, your favorite lamp and a TV tray for writing, whatever makes you feel pampered.

CONSIDERATIONS

- Stock your getaway room so that you use it. A scrapbook room should be equipped with stickers, albums, scissors, glue and markers. In the same respect, a gift wrapping room is incomplete without a closet full of presents, wrapping paper, ribbon, gift cards, tape and scissors—everything you need to wrap gifts—and the necessities for mailing them.

- Think about your family's interests. Do these pursuits warrant their own room? If so, options might include a children's television room, husband's sports room, workout room or a meditation/chi room.

Some Best Things Come...SMALL

A small space requires planning and demands smart choices.
Here's the inside scoop on making an area appear roomier:

- Paint the room's walls, ceiling and large pieces of furniture in the same light shade to unify the space.

- Use semi-gloss paint to reflect light.

- Paint the ceiling an accent color.

- Keep the floor treatment the same throughout. If it has a pattern, e.g., tile flooring, lay it on the diagonal.

- For a clean, uncluttered, spacious look, go with a wooden floor.

- Use furniture sparingly. Note: White furniture magnifies the area.

- Select corner pieces of furniture, those that neatly tuck into the walls or built-ins. And use space saving furnishings, such as tables with fold-down leaves.

- Consider multi-task furniture, such as an accent stool that doubles as a side table or a chair that converts to a stepladder.

- Maximize a small bedroom space with a daybed or a bed with storage stylishly built in beneath it.

- Make prime use of your vertical space. Layer toward the ceiling, using shelves for display, as well as for storage. Leading the eye upward creates a larger illusion.

- Add drama with a chandelier, though it must be a small chandelier.

- Don't forget mirrors to expand the space.

- Use color to accent.

- Make a statement!

FOUR

COLOR IT, LAYER IT, ADD PATTERNS

$\mathcal{L}$ike the ingredients of a cherished family recipe . . . colors, layers and patterns best mold a house into your home. Add texture to this mix and you have an unbeatable combination.

In the decorating world, this is the fun part. Get ready to have a good time!

SPLASHED IN COLOR

The color requisite is not whether it's trendy or popular but if it's right for you and your family. To know if a color will work for you and to use it appropriately, learn how color affects you. Here's a bit of color psychology.

> ### White
> ---
> TRANSLATION
> ---
> **FRESH,
> CLEAN,
> PURE**

$\mathcal{W}$hite is not a single color but a combination of all colors. It is a simple selection because it is easily combined with any color. When used as an accent, white creates contrast (e.g., baseboards and window trim in a dark room or piping on a colored upholstered piece). White makes everything else stand out. But take note: White never cozies up a space.

Technically not a color, pure black is actually the absence of color. According to many decorators, black is the one choice that should be found in every room. I agree (I additionally try to incorporate a touch of red). If used in the right amounts, black can be an effective accent. It provides a rich contrast. But if used as a dominate color, do so with guidance. Black is favored by men—it's a strong color, not a feminine one.

Black

TRANSLATION

UPSCALE, MODERN, SOPHISTICATED, EVOKES WEALTH

Brown

TRANSLATION

**EARTHY,
SIMPLE,
WARM**

While very dark brown is sometimes used as a substitution for black, brown is more casual than its cosmopolitan counterpart. Found abundantly in nature it is a warm, neutral color that projects a wholesome, honest feel. Brown is used more often to enhance a fall and winter look than for summer or spring, though when paired with white it works well in the warmer seasons.

Red is a wonderful accent. This happy color has distinguishing characteristics: Red makes you less aware of time, looks especially good at night and stimulates the appetite—making it a popular choice for dining rooms. Red is the first color babies see (consider its use in the nursery for stimulation . . . in moderation). However, because of its aggressive quality, it's not the best choice for a teen's room. Though strong, the color can be toned down with shades of green and blue-green (colors opposite on the color wheel). Red is another top choice of men.

Red

TRANSLATION

**ENERGETIC,
PASSIONATE,
SEXY,
POWERFUL,
HOT**

natural color found in the sky and sea, blue is an all-American favorite. Almost everyone likes some shade of blue. But though the color is always in style, it's never the same blue . . . so beware of shades that are trendy. The color's cool, peaceful effect makes time pass more quickly—it even makes you sleep better—making it a good choice for a bedroom. However, blue is easy to tire of and too much of this color can border on boring.

Blue

TRANSLATION

**CALMING,
SOOTHING,
NURTURING**

Green is a warm, restful color with some of the same calming attributes of blue. Green is life. Abundant in nature, green signifies growth, renewal and spring. Because green is the easiest color for the eye to see, it is effectively used as a neutral. Green is a favorite of both men and women.

Green

TRANSLATION

**REFRESHING,
RELAXING,
SERENE**

Yellow

TRANSLATION

**HAPPY,
SUNNY,
VIBRANT**

The color of the sun, yellow suggests new beginnings. It's a good color to use in a poorly lit area. Though the color projects cheery warmth, beware that bright yellow can cause anxiety if displayed in large areas. It is also the most attention-getting color, so a small dose of yellow can make a powerful impact (e.g., a vase of yellow flowers). Note of interest: Yellow houses typically sell first.

This flamboyant color is tough to use and can be a fad choice. Your best bet is to select orange as an accent. Orange (and rust, a variation of the color) can be found in nature—fall leaves, the setting sun and citrus fruit. It represents the changing seasons—images of autumn. It's a great party color, especially when mixed with bright pinks and greens.

Orange

TRANSLATION

**EXCITING,
ENERGETIC,
STIMULATING**

Other than used as an accent, purple is a difficult color to apply in interior design. Why? Purple can be a challenge to combine with other colors. Tip: It works best in soft hues and with white, green, blue or pink. Deep or bright purples project prosperity, while lilacs and violets are delicate color selections. And purple is not a good color choice for re-sale.

Purple

TRANSLATION

**ROYAL,
NOBLE,
SPIRITUAL**

Though technically not a color, this neutral hue provides a relaxing backdrop if seeking a neat, tidy look. But though the benefit of beige may be a clean palette, beware of a look that can be uninteresting. The antidote to this potential dilemma is to pair it with texture or color. It provides the perfect backdrop for a collection. Known as a dependable and flexible choice, beige has been called the chameleon of colors, taking on attributes of whichever pigment it is paired.

Beige

TRANSLATION

**TRANQUIL,
SAFE,
TRADITIONAL**

Gray is a neutral, balanced color. Calming to the eye, it is a cool, conservative choice. Gray is associated with metal; its use imparts a high-end image. However, pay attention to the shade of gray you select—some grays can be depressing.

Gray

TRANSLATION

SLEEK, CONTEMPORARY, COSMOPOLITAN

COURTING COLOR

Does the thought of putting together a color scheme terrify you? To many, the answer is "yes." Because my business is to combine colors, I've often wondered why this is so— I think it may be because you're afraid to make a mistake. You don't think you are good at it, and you don't want to fail.

My advice is straight forward. Study color—it's fun. Then experiment, experiment, experiment—until you get it right. After a while, success will come from skill, no longer from trial and error. It's exciting when it works!

CONSIDERATIONS

- Room-by-room: make a color statement with your entry; have fun with colors in your dining room; decorate a bedroom for relaxation (pass over dark colors for a pastel hue).

- Start with something you love in the room to devise a color scheme (e.g., the hint of grass green in your grandmother's teapot, hot pink of the Gerber daisy featured in a colorful print or the hues of a favorite floral arrangement).

- Look no further than your windows when creating a paint palette. If the view is an irresistible landscape, continue it into your home with similar colors—they will also extend your space.

- Think of a fond locale and duplicate those colors in your home. For example, if your family's favorite vacation was to the South of France, use daffodil yellow and Provencal blue.

- Don't negate white because it's boring—there are hundreds of shades of white. A white room gives you a clean slate—a space to have fun with color in upholstery, bedding, artwork, window frames and accessories.

- If a colored wall is out of your comfort zone, substitute a buttery yellow for the standard white. Then, you can incorporate color on the doors, moldings and baseboards.

- For a creative statement, paint the trim around a room's doors and windows a darker color, even a contrasting one.

- Go for it! Accent colors are easily changed—candles can be burned, pillows recovered, picture frames replaced.

THUMBNAIL SKETCH

The general rule of thumb is to combine one warm color (red, yellow, orange) with one cool color (blue, green, purple). An effective example of this warm/cool color combination is the popular and patriotic red and blue palette. Another pleasing blend is red and green. Though best known as the standard Christmas duo, the color combination is also a nurturing year-round choice.

How can you subtly incorporate this principle into your home? Alternate warm and cool shades from one room to the next (example: a warm-color entry leading into a cool-color living room). The result will be a color scheme of calm. Keep in mind that warm colors make a room seem warmer (temperature-wise) and cool colors provide the opposite effect, so a warm hue might not be the best kitchen choice.

But you don't have to go by the rules. You can decorate with all warm or all cool colors. Do what you like!

And if you are unsure of colors that go together, take your cues from nature and those combos found in florals, animals or the sea. All are great palette guides, such as the orange and purple union of the bird-of-paradise flower. Refer to the artwork of the masters, e.g., the blue, green and pink composition found in Claude Monet's water lily paintings. Or look out your window and match your exterior view. Remember, anything goes.

Combine one warm color with one cool color.

BREAKING THE COLOR CODE

If you remain color confused, consider the following:

- Color is an inexpensive way to add warmth, create drama and set a mood.

- The cheapest use of color is paint. It's the easiest way to change the personality of a room.

- The focal point of a room can be color (e.g., red and black décor in a light beige room).

- Add color in your kitchen with a distinctive tile backsplash.

- Go with pale versus bright color to tone down a sun-filled area.

- To create a sense of space, paint the walls a neutral color.

- To create a cozy room, paint the walls a darker color.

- Contrasting colors make spaces more intriguing because they create visual interest, such as a beige room and red baseboards. (The most extreme example is a white room accented with black baseboards, window frames and doors.)

COLOR MATTERS

Because color evokes mood, understand its properties
and use it advantageously.

Nurture

pastel shades of yellows, pinks and peaches with
soothing whites and muted greens

Romantic

delicate blend of colors punctuated by reds and pinks

Sensuous

bold reds and purples

Tranquil

soft blues, lavenders and subtle greens

Whimsical

combination of vivid and dissimilar, shocking
or unexpected colors (example: carousel horse in
assorted bright colors serving as the centerpiece of
your child's room)

PAINT THE CEILING A SHADE OR TWO LIGHTER
THAN THE WALLS. OR ACCENT NEUTRAL OR WHITE
WALLS WITH A COLORED CEILING. KEEP IN MIND
THAT A DARK COLORED CEILING WILL MAKE
IT APPEAR LOWER.

PACK IT WITH PATTERNS—
TEAM IT WITH TEXTURE

Pattern and texture are the decorating duo responsible for interest and character in an otherwise plain color scheme. Continuing the "recipe" analogy, these elements are the seasoning—as essential to the look of your home as spices are to your food.

Use this twosome on your walls, floors or furniture. Strive toward a smart mix and the visual result will be vitality.

PATTERN PERFECT

Patterns are versatile. They can be painted onto furniture, added to walls with wallpaper and incorporated into fabrics through prints.

BUT WHEN IT COMES TO PATTERNS, NOTE THESE PRINCIPLES:

- *Vertical lines* add height to a room, making stripes advisable in a short room and discouraged in a tall, narrow area.

- *Horizontal lines* add space and width to an area.

- *Stripes* are a classic way to bring energy to your look.

- Think *size and scale*. Informal rule: the larger the space, the larger the print; the smaller the space, the smaller the print. Yet, adding a large print to a small area can give the look of grandeur, especially if it is an open, airy design. Conversely, a small print can bring formality to a large area. Your choice depends on the amount of punch you seek. (The same guidelines apply to upholstered furniture.)

- Revisit *size and scale*. Decide purpose. Will the pattern enhance a designated anchor, such as a sofa or recliner (showy and significant) or be defined as background (small and subtle)? Beware that undersized, busy patterns may cause a dizzy effect, so make sure your print selection doesn't create an odd visual sensation.

- *Color* affects how we see *patterns*. High contrast patterns create an energetic environment; colors close in value project a more subdued feel.

- *Different patterns* can be complementary if they are of similar scale (e.g., a bold striped print paired with an oversized checked pattern).

- The key to putting together a *variety of patterns* is using a similar color scheme.

- Consider the *versatility of animal print*—its graphic pattern not only makes a striking statement but works just about anywhere (much like a neutral). Incorporate it into your décor through an accent welt on a chair's upholstery, the fringe on your draperies or a single sofa pillow.

High contrast patterns create an energetic environment...

THINK TEXTURE

To grasp the importance of texture as an interior design tool, imagine a room with none—completely smooth surfaces, no pattern in fabrics, no trim on upholstery or pillows, no carved wooden doors—plain flat walls and a ceiling to match. Even if filled with color, one glance around a texture-free room would translate to dull. Right?

This is because texture is the decorating element you see and touch—it is visual and tactile.

Examples of rough textures are many: linoleum flooring, molded textured glass, worsted wool, rough sawn timber, brick, wicker furniture, sisal carpeting, plaster walls, even a fur throw.

Conversely, samples of smooth textures include glass, chrome, plastic, lacquer paint finish, leather, vinyl upholstery, chintz fabric, black granite, polished brass and more.

And texture affects color. Rough textures add warmth and absorb light; smooth textures add coolness and reflect light.

TEXTURES TALK

The feel of a room parallels the textures used in it. Texture significantly impacts how moods are made and emotions are honed. Rough textures make rooms seem smaller, cozier, nostalgic, richer in history and more casual. Whereas, rooms with high gloss and smooth textures appear larger, colder, more sophisticated and dramatic.

Decorate for the style you seek. Here are some texture details to help you create the atmosphere where you want to live.

- OPEN LOOK – Use smooth, plain textures.

- COZY LOOK – Consider soft, fuzzy, jagged, velvet and fibrous textures.

- FORMAL LOOK – Think about grid and straight line textures.

- DOWN TO EARTH LOOK – Among your texture choices are fibers, weaves, wicker, rough surfaces and brick.

ADDING TEXTURE CAN BE AS SIMPLE AS EMBELLISHING ITEMS SUCH AS PILLOWS, LAMPSHADES AND CURTAINS WITH TASSELS, BEADS OR FRINGE.

TEXTURE TIP

Where the cohesive use of texture creates harmony, mixing several without context to one another can translate to a disjointed design. So, before pairing textures, think about your choices.

Consider the look of pairing a wicker chair with a sculpted carpet. Would the textures complement one another? Or would they compete? I say they would compete (used in combo, each would cancel the other item's special effect). But this is my opinion. To determine your own, use the above complement/compete exercise throughout the decorating process.

And don't neglect the value of greenery—plants can soften edges and act as hole fillers.

FOLLOW-UP WITH FABRICS

Like colors, a textile projects a distinct personality that is expressed through its texture.

Fabrics talk. They can say "welcome," adding "come and sit" or communicate "look but don't touch." To better educate you and help you achieve your desired message, here are some fabric facts:

Brocade
RICH, FANCY, FORMAL

Chintz
CLEAN, FRESH, SIMPLE, COUNTRY

Corduroy
DURABLE, CASUAL, COLD-WEATHER COMFORT

Gingham
COUNTRY, INFORMAL (THOUGH THE FORMALITY OF THE LOOK DEPENDS ON THE SIZE OF THE PRINT) EXAMPLE: RALPH LAUREN'S LARGE, BOLD CHECKS SAY SOPHISTICATION.

Lace
DELICATE, FEMININE, AIRY, ROMANTIC

Leather
MASCULINE, CONTEMPORARY, TIMELESS

Organza
GLAMOROUS, DRAMATIC (ESPECIALLY WHEN USED AS AN ACCENT AND IN LAYERS)

Silk
RICH, FOREVER, TIMELESS, SOPHISTICATED

Tapestry
FORMAL, OLD WORLD, TUSCAN

Velvet
LUXURIOUS, HEAVY, WARM

LATHER ON THE LAYERS

Whether framing a wall of windows with custom shades and yards of
shimmery silk, covering a chenille couch with an embroidered shawl
or piling a bed with accent pillows, all bring personality to your living
spaces. All add interest and depth. And all represent layering.

Layering is not exclusive to texture. You can layer with color
(brown bed linens, topped with a red duvet and accented with yellow
and green pillows). You also layer with patterns (a pink floral sofa,
accented with contrasting print pillows).

You can layer with patterns...

You can layer with accessories...

But don't forget accessories. Learn to layer them, too. Let's say you start with colorful artwork and distinctive candlesticks. Perhaps you want to add a topiary and framed photograph, along with other favorite items. Place them in position one at a time, stepping back to make an assessment after each inclusion. Add a bit here and subtract a piece there. Use your innate sense of design. Allow your eye to tell you what feels right. Take your time. Continue to evaluate and re-evaluate, layer by layer. Note: Layer in uneven numbers, whether it's three, five, seven, nine or another odd quantity of items.

Lastly, ascribe to this adage: Don't be afraid. There's no need. In the process of reading this book, you've begun to understand the principles of design. From this moment forward, decorate from education, not intimidation.

FIVE

EVERY DAY, EVERY LOOK, EVERY SEASON

*H*omes do more than talk. They tell stories, though not always the same story. Your home transforms with time—as your family evolves, your interests change and the years progress. There's no magic here. The key is to continually make a house your home as your life moves forward.

DOWNSIZE YOUR DIGS

Scaling down is a common theme these days, whether it's a natural reaction to your kids leaving home, your retirement, a divorce or just wanting a simpler lifestyle. Going smaller is easier than you might think if you keep only the pieces you really like and strive to streamline. And in the case of a divorce, pay even more attention to making your place homey and making it yours.

SUBURBAN VS. URBAN

SUBURBAN A residential enclave is typically slower-paced, cushy, washable and durable. The suburban house is about family. It is home; it represents roots. This house is not just a place where your family showers and sleeps. It is a playful yard and swing set, a beckoning family room and an inviting kitchen. It is where memories are made.

URBAN Designed for low maintenance and efficiency, lofts attract those with a city dweller's mindset who enjoy a fast-paced lifestyle, are no longer married to home and have a new-found freedom. This is a home where space is a premium and you've splurged on your fabrics and furniture (the by-product of a child-free dwelling).

How is the transition made from suburban to urban? Decorating for function provides the solution to success. Whether you decorate your loft as a cozy cottage with smaller-scale furnishings or create a sleek modern look, consider the three m's—modular, maximized views and multi-functional furniture (e.g., a dining room table doubling as your work desk).

Here's some insight into decorating for function and fashion:

- Strive for an expansive feeling, e.g., an open space with few walls. Use furniture (even the headboard of your bed) to make "walls."

- Incorporate bookcases, half-walls, screens and distinctive rugs to form individual areas within a broad space.

- Select furniture with strong architectural lines, fine sculptural quality and personality to make a statement of your style.

- And select furniture conducive to open space. Use pieces that look good from all angles. Maintain unobstructed views—go with backless bookcases, chairs with open arms and coffee tables with see-through shelves. Scale furniture to the room.

- Organize, organize, organize. A loft has no room for clutter. Create storage in armoires or custom design under-the-bed space for off-season clothing.

- Decorate around a dramatic color scheme. Have no fear that it will overpower (its effect is diluted by the surrounding open-air space).

FROM COOL
TO COMFORT

TO TRANSFORM A DOWNTOWN LOFT FROM
URBAN COOL TO COUNTRY-LIKE COMFORT:
SPRINKLE IT WITH GREENERY,
INCORPORATE WICKER ELEMENTS
AND ADD COZY THROWS AND PILLOWS
TO SOFTEN THE LOOK.

LOOKS AND LOCATION

It's common for interior design to reflect your geographical area. In my locale, for instance, California décor is typically casual, like its lifestyle. Note that if the kind of lifestyle you seek does not represent where you live, you can reproduce it anywhere. However, it should always fit quietly into the environs.

ARCHITECTURAL INSPIRATION

NEW MEXICO
Adobe, Native American

DOWNTOWN SAN FRANCISCO
Victorian

NORTH AND SOUTH CAROLINA
Cottage homes

SOUTHERN CALIFORNIA
Mexican, beach influence

MY LOOK FOR MY LOCATION

Being a Southern Californian, it should be no surprise that my beach house follows a coastal theme.

Low-key comfort typifies beach style. The easiest way to create a seaside décor is to start with a color scheme suggested by nature: sea blues, foamy whites and sandy tans. Combine these hues with natural fibers, simple artwork and scattered collections of seashells, sea glass, and bleached driftwood. The result is California casual.

Spring Clean up. To assist the arrival of spring, transform your winter retreat to a mood of renewal — organize your home and plant your garden. Replace slipcovers and change the pillows for the season. Repaint wicker furniture that needs to be freshened up. Exchange your cold weather bedding for airy coverings in softer tones. Take your inspiration from nature (consider florals, botanically-inspired prints or rattan furnishings).

Summer Lighten up. As temperatures rise, it seems only natural to "summerize" a home. So swap out any remaining heavy drapery panels for matchstick blinds or sheers. Remove area rugs and leave your floors bare or go with natural fiber rugs. Fill your home with fresh flowers. They'll brighten your rooms, as well as your mood.

Fall Cozy up. Seasonal scents capture the essence of autumn (cinnamon, bayberry and currant). Surround yourself with aromas. This is also the time to decorate with nature's own ornaments, such as pinecones, acorns and bird nests. Replace your flower motifs with leaf-inspired accessories.

Winter Hunker down. This is the time of year to prepare for the onslaught of inclement weather and the transition to shorter days and cozier nights. It's the season to settle in. But it's also the time to dress your home for the holidays.

IN THE SPIRIT OF SUMMER, DECORATE A TREE WITH SEASONAL "ACCESSORIES," SUCH AS SAND PAILS, SHOVELS AND FLIP FLOPS. OR TURN THE YARD'S TREE HOUSE INTO A SUMMERTIME PLAYHOUSE.

OPPOSITE

Same family room with spring (above) and fall (below) decorating touches.

"HOME" FOR
THE HOLIDAYS

Your goal for any holiday should be a home that greets everyone who steps through your door with warmth. Easy transformations are made with wreaths, placemats, centerpieces, dishes, lights, sounds, seasonal flags and decorative trees. Each holiday has its own look, its own theme, its own purpose. Let's see how they can differ, starting with the grandest holiday of all—Christmas.

· Christmas ·

Considered by many to be the biggest day of the year, Christmas is about holiday spirit and everyone—young and old. Christmas is: the nativity, Santa, trees, tradition, sparkling lights, holly berries, festive carols and holiday magic. Colors: red, green, gold and silver (I'm a purist when it comes to Christmas colors). Foliage: poinsettias.

PICTURE THIS...

- Make custom wall art from a weathered piece of wood and a stenciled seasonal saying, such as "Be naughty: Save Santa the trip" or "Dear Santa: I tried."

- Frame a doorway with garland and display Christmas cards within the greenery.

- Establish your color theme and then choose plaids or florals that tie in.

- Think beyond the wreath on your front door that greets visitors. Also display one inside your entry door to wish your guests a "Merry Christmas" as they leave your home, too. I additionally use wreaths on all the windows, inside and out.

- Make your own handcrafted Christmas wreath. Decorate it with holiday ribbons and ornaments or get funky. A personal favorite is to use Christmas soaps on a wreath in my powder room.

- Always, always, always use fresh wreaths and garlands to bring seasonal fragrance into your holiday décor. Think along the lines of eucalyptus or fresh evergreens with berries and pinecones.

- Weave strands of glass beads among your decorative table accessories.

- Decorate your stairway with potted plants. This only works if your stairs are wide enough to allow for safe passage to walk up and down them. Place poinsettias, small potted Christmas trees or other greenery on alternating steps. Add holiday bows to match your color scheme.

- Bring Christmas to any foliage already in your home. Example: Set a Santa at the base of a plant.

- Use holiday tableware for every meal in December.

- Start a set of holiday dishes with dinner plates that coordinate with your everyday dishes. Add new pieces every Christmas, such as salad plates and mugs; but be sure the pattern will be continued from year to year. If you buy one or two place settings each season, it won't be long before you're able to serve a feast.

- Look through your cupboards and use every dish that looks festive. Take note that discount stores often carry seconds of name-brand china, as well as fun designs that are not so common.

- Buy one place setting of a different pattern each year if you're adventuresome. Use the unmatched dishes every Christmas, setting both an eclectic holiday table and one that revisits the memories of past years.

- Make a dining room table centerpiece by turning a collection of silver, brass, or glass candleholders into vases, topping each piece with a beautiful ornament.

- Attach a small sprig of cedar to a napkin ring. Select a shape that replicates a small Christmas tree; tie a ribbon into a bow at its base.

- Wrap your door like a Christmas present with heavy foil gift wrapping paper. Complete the look with extra-wide ribbon extending from the four sides of the door to the center, accented with a big bow.

- Look in every room for the potential to make it Christmas. Children love to have their rooms decorated. Hang a wreath on the bedroom door or over the bed. Personalize it with your child's name or decorate it in a theme close to their heart, such as music, sports, pets or just Christmas. Everybody loves Christmas!

THOUGH YOUR MANTEL IS THE STANDARD BEARER OF STOCKINGS, STUFF A DECORATIVE STOCKING WITH CANDY CANES, EVERGREENS AND A SMALL TOY AND HANG IT ON THE FRONT DOOR IN PLACE OF A WREATH. AS YOUR FAMILY GROWS TO INCLUDE IN-LAWS AND GRANDCHILDREN, THERE IS NOTHING WRONG WITH MIX-AND-MATCH (OR MIX-AND-DON'T MATCH) CHRISTMAS STOCKINGS.

CHRISTMAS
SPIRIT

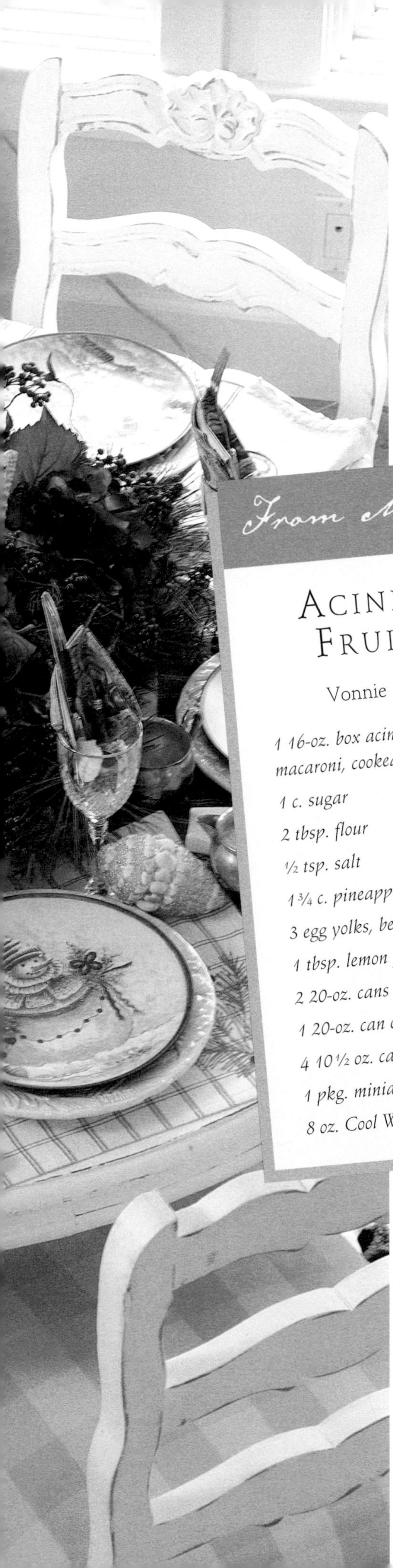

My family doesn't consider it a legitimate get-together unless we have acini di pepe fruit salad. It's simply a staple at our holiday celebrations.

From My Kitchen...and My Heart!

Acini Di Pepe Fruit Salad

Vonnie McMillin, mother

1 16-oz. box acini di pepe macaroni, cooked
1 c. sugar
2 tbsp. flour
½ tsp. salt
1¾ c. pineapple juice
3 egg yolks, beaten
1 tbsp. lemon juice
2 20-oz. cans pineapple chunks, drained
1 20-oz. can crushed pineapple, drained
4 10½ oz. cans Mandarin oranges, drained
1 pkg. miniature marshmallows
8 oz. Cool Whip, thawed

Cook macaroni in salted water: drain and set aside.

Mix together sugar, flour, salt, pineapple juice, egg yolks and lemon juice.

Cook over medium heat, stirring constantly, until thickened.

Cool completely. Add macaroni.

May be refrigerated overnight (Note: I use a large sealed Tupperware container).

Add well-drained pineapple and oranges. Then add marshmallows and Cool Whip. Refrigerate before seving.

Feeds a large crowd!

Use holiday tableware for every meal in December.

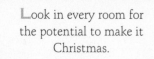

Look in every room for
the potential to make it
Christmas.

ON THE FIRST DAY OF CHRISTMAS...

Holiday traditions. They vary from family to family. Our holidays are all day celebrations. We begin with a big breakfast, followed by a buffet lunch and end the day with a lavish dinner. Christmas Eve is always at my mom's. Christmas Day is at my house.

What are your holiday traditions? If you are looking to add new ones or are just starting out and want to begin with your own customs, these ideas may just get you inspired. By having a few standard traditions, you may find yourself looking even more forward to Christmas as the season rolls around.

Start a Book of Traditions. Purchase a beautifully bound blank book with acid-free pages. In it, record everything about each Christmas holiday. Note the year, where you lived (helpful if you move frequently), what the tree looked like, traditions you observed and who was there. Ask guests and visitors to write a few lines as well. Record special gifts received and those given. Include photos of the tree, your family and your guests in the book.

Put a Date on the Calendar. Pick a time to put up your Christmas tree every year. It can be the Friday after Thanksgiving, December 1st, the first weekend in December—whenever you choose. Make it your holiday tradition to always decorate your tree on this designated date. Treat it as a special night. Dress for the occasion, serve Christmas cookies and "dress" the tree at leisure, all the while sipping champagne or eggnog.

Show Time. Help the younger family members showcase their Thespian skills by staging a play for holiday entertainment. Rehearse through the month of December. Curtain is Christmas Day. The play can always be the same or a different choice each year; and it can be as elaborate or as informal as your energy dictates.

Same Time Next Year. Give the children pajamas every Christmas Eve. Make it your tradition for them to wear this gift to bed that evening, after hearing Dad's annual recitation of 'Twas the Night Before Christmas.

HOW TO DECORATE
YOUR CHRISTMAS TREE

Would you like for your Christmas tree to have a designer look? Start with a well-shaped tree; ideally, it should brush the ceiling. The secret is a multi-step layer process. Lights, garland, ornaments, action—let's get going.

Lights! Your tree's lights are its most important element—they provide a sparkling background to showcase your ornaments. Illuminate the tree from the inside out by stringing the lights from the base of the trunk and working up and out to every tip of a branch (and back again to the trunk).

Be liberal with lights! For every vertical foot of tree, use a strand of 100 lights. And don't be afraid to mix and match lights. There's no rule stating that you can only use one kind—a mixture adds interest.

Garland! Start at the top with the garland and work your way down the tree (the amount of garland increases as you go). Guideline: Use about two strands of garland for every vertical foot of tree.

Smaller bead garlands look best swagged from branch to branch; thicker versions (e.g., paper, ribbon and foil) work well when wrapped loosely around the entire tree. It's always fun to string popcorn with the kids and let them decorate with their home-cooked garland.

Don't be afraid—just go with it.

Ornaments! Begin with your most important ornaments; place them in prime spots on the tree. Follow with the largest ornaments and space them evenly. Fill in the holes with medium- and small-sized pieces to balance the look. Finish with specialty shapes. To create depth, hang some ornaments close to the trunk.

Consider a themed tree. Use family heirlooms (such as silver baby cups) for a silver-inspired tree or decorate with sea shells and sea glass ornaments for one that is ocean-influenced—my family's tree always has teddy bears, snowmen and oversized Santas. Or you can simply celebrate the natural beauty of your tree with clear glass balls.

Action! Everything goes. You can't have too many trees, too much on them or too much fun. Enjoy your Christmas tree, enjoy the holidays, enjoy your family!

Thanksgiving

This time of year represents the pure appreciation of family. Thanksgiving is: turkeys, pilgrims, cornucopia, gourds, corn husks and fall leaves. Colors: rust, brown, orange, amber, copper and gold. Foliage: orange tulips, crab apples and rosehips.

PICTURE THIS...

- Use nature to make an autumn centerpiece. Think about what you find on pathways or in your backyard. It can be as simple as a bowl of pine cones surrounded by fall leaves and punctuated by a handful of colorful twigs. Or go with some small pumpkins and ears of dried corn, garnished with a twig bird's nest.

- Gather bouquets of fall leaves for vases and fill wooden or ceramic bowls with pinecones, gourds and Indian corn. Place these decorative accents all around your home.

- Fill a platter with fruit and flowers of the same color, such as artichokes (to match the greenery) paired with lemons and daisies. Note: Ripening fruit can cause fresh flowers to wilt, so add flowers only an hour or so before guests arrive. Most flowers will last a couple of hours out of water; or use florist water tubes to keep flowers fresh for a few days.

- Create a dining room table arrangement with your choice of silver, brass or crystal vases, bowls, compotes and candleholders in a variety of heights; and accent with beaded fruit. Or go with silver items and replace the beaded fruit with real touches from nature, such as grapes, pumpkins or squash—painted silver. An ornate sterling serving tray will complete the look.

- Replace your traditional turkey accessories with leaf-patterned décor in colors that echo those of your Thanksgiving table.

- Use pine cones to hold place cards. Or simply tie a ribbon around a selection of artificial flowers and add a name tag.

- Make candleholders by hollowing out some apples and placing a votive candle in the center of each.

OPPOSITE
Tie a ribbon around a selection of artificial flowers and add a name tag.

BELOW
Hollow out some apples and place a votive candle in each.

- Fill a clear vase with fresh cranberries; add budding red flowers (I like anemones). Or go with orange-and-yellow candy corn paired with sunflowers.

This recipe was passed down to my family from my grandmother, my mother's mom. She lived in Westby, a very small town in Montana, where everything was homegrown and homemade.

From My Kitchen...and My Heart!

ORANGE CAKE

Grandma Leininger

2 c. flour

1 tsp. baking soda

Pinch salt

2 eggs

1 ½ c. sugar

1 ½ c. sour cream

1 orange

1 c. raisins

Sift together flour, baking soda and salt and set aside.

Blend eggs with sugar and sour cream.

Grind entire orange (rind and pulp) with raisins and add to egg/sugar mixture.

Gradually add dry ingredients to creamed mixture, blending thoroughly.

Pour into well-greased and lightly floured 13 x 9 x 2-inch pan.

Bake at 350° for approximately 45 minutes (until a toothpick inserted into the center of the cake comes out clean and dry).

Let cake cool to room temperature.

FROSTING:

½ c. butter (1 stick), room temperature

8-oz. pkg. cream cheese, room temperature

2–3 c. powdered sugar

1 tsp. vanilla extract

With an electric mixer, blend together the butter and cream cheese; approximately 3 minutes on medium speed until very smooth.

Add the vanilla extract and mix.

Slowly add the powdered sugar, continuing until you get the desired sweetness.

Use a blunt knife or spatula to spread the frosting onto your cake.

OPPOSITE

Use real touches from nature, such as straw and pine cones.

Valentine's Day

Romance defines this day. Valentine's Day is: hearts, cupids, bows and arrows. Colors: red, pink and white. Foliage: roses. Food and drink: heart-shaped sugar cookies, chilled champagne and anything chocolate (from fudge brownies to chocolate martinis).

PICTURE THIS . . .

- Plan a picnic for two in front of the fireplace.

- Schedule a surprise horse-and-buggy ride.

- Scatter decorative bowls of Valentine candies throughout the house.

Early on, our family began to look forward to every occasion because Darcie would bring her brownies. It continues to this day.

From My Kitchen...and My Heart!

DARCIE'S BROWNIES

Darcie, cousin's wife

¾ c. Hershey's cocoa

½ tsp. baking soda

⅔ c. vegetable oil (divide into two equal portions)

½ c. boiling water

2 c. sugar

2 eggs

1 ½ c. flour

1 tsp. vanilla

¼ tsp. salt

1 c. walnuts

Preheat oven to 350°F.

Grease 13 x 9 x 2-inch baking pan.

In medium bowl, stir together cocoa and baking soda; blend in ⅓ cup vegetable oil.

Add boiling water; stir until mixture thickens.

Blend in sugar, eggs and remaining ⅓ cup vegetable oil; stirring until smooth.

Add flour, vanilla and salt; blend well. Stir in walnuts.

Pour into prepared pan. Bake 35–45 minutes.

Cool; then add frosting.

Makes about 36 brownies.

FROSTING

1 c. sugar

¼ c. milk

¼ c. margarine

1 tsp. vanilla

1 c. chocolate chips (½ c. milk chocolate chips; ½ c. semi-sweet chocolate chips)

Combine sugar, milk and margarine; bring to a boil for 1 minute.

Add vanilla and chocolate chips and beat until smooth.

Spread the frosting on cooled brownies in the pan.

LAT

CONTINUE YOUR HOUSE'S RED CHRISTMAS THEME (SANS TREE AND SANTAS) INTO FEBRUARY. TO DECORATE FOR VALENTINE'S DAY, SIMPLY REPLACE YOUR GREEN DÉCOR WITH WHITE OR PINK SUBSTITUTIONS.

LAT

IGNORE THE "COUPLES ONLY" TRADITION FOR VALENTINE'S DAY AND MAKE IT A FAMILY OCCASION WITH HOMEMADE CARDS AND A "WEAR ANYTHING RED" MOM, DAD AND KIDS' DINNER. INCLUDE EVERYONE IN THIS HOLIDAY, CELEBRATE IT TWICE: FAMILY NIGHT AND A ROMANTIC EVENING FOR TWO.

Easter

Though the actual date varies from year to year, spring unofficially begins with this holiday. Easter is: bunnies, bonnets, eggs and egg hunts. Colors: pastel pinks, purples, greens, blues and yellows. Foliage: tulips, hydrangeas and lilies. Food: baked ham and gelatin salads.

PICTURE THIS . . .

- Appeal to the kid in everyone at your Easter brunch by setting each place with a chocolate bunny and a pastel-colored seating card decorated with floral stickers.

- Pull your vintage teacups and saucers from your cupboards and use them as containers for tiny flower arrangements to brighten kitchen counters, bedside tables or powder rooms. Fill the cups with well-soaked floral foam and use small blooms, such as grape hyacinth, lily of the valley, snowdrop or crocus, to match the scale of the cups.

- Fill tiny wire baskets with peat moss or Easter grass, along with a handful of colored foil-wrapped candies. Finish the baskets with big bows made from silk wire-edge ribbon and attach to dining room chair backs with twine, tying them tightly to ensure the baskets don't sag.

- Set white dinner plates on a white linen tablecloth. Add color: green salad plates, pink glasses and fresh purple tulips to be used as holders for your place cards.

- Make your own place card holders by painting small terra cotta flowerpots with a pastel shade of acrylic paint. Fill the pots with Easter grass or another color of tissue paper and top them with candy. Nestle the place card in the candy atop the flowerpot.

- Turn old bud vases or candlestick holders into seasonal works of art. With very little paint, tiny strokes of color will transform your plain glassware. Use paint pens in desired colors and widths (available at an arts and crafts store) to decorate with vertical or horizontal lines and small designs, such as flowers.

LA

MAKE UNCONVENTIONAL EASTER BASKETS. I'VE FILLED MY GIRLS' BASKETS WITH GIFTS SUCH AS FLIP FLOPS, SWIMSUITS, SWIM GOGGLES, EVEN BEACH TOWELS. AND MY SON'S EASTER THEMED TREAT HAS BEEN A PAINTED WAGON STUFFED WITH BASEBALL GEAR, STICKERS AND BABY RUTH CANDY BARS.

Many of our family recipes come from my relatives' church pot-luck-dinner days in Plentywood, Montana.

MARIANNE'S JELL-O

. . . .

Marianne, aunt

1 3 oz. pkg. Jell-O (your choice of flavors; I use one that reflects the season)

2 c. water

1 3¼ oz. box Americana tapioca pudding (not instant)

1 c. whipping cream (whipped yielding 2 cups) or 8 oz. Cool Whip, thawed

1 tsp. vanilla

1 tbsp. powdered sugar

Bring to a boil water, Jell-O and tapioca, stirring constantly.

Refrigerate until partially thickened.

Fold in Cool Whip, vanilla and powdered sugar.

Continue to refrigerate until set.

Makes 8 to 10 servings.

BROCCOLI SALAD

. . . .

Vonnie McMillin, mother

4 c. fresh broccoli crowns

½ c. Miracle Whip

3 tbsp. sugar

1 tbsp. cider vinegar

1 c. sunflower seeds

1 c. dark raisins

½ c. red onion (sliced)

10 strips cooked bacon, crumbled

Chop broccoli crowns to bite-size pieces.

Mix Miracle Whip, vinegar and sugar.

Pour over broccoli. Add sunflower seeds, raisins, onion and bacon.

Mix well. Refrigerate.

· July 4th ·

America's Independence Day is marked by around-the-nation patriotic displays. July 4th is: American flags, bike parades, picnics, red-and-white gingham tablecloths and sights and sounds of fireworks. Colors: red, white and blue. Foliage: daisies, red tulips and white tulips. Food and drink: tasty barbeque, hot dogs and cold lemonade.

PICTURE THIS...

- Add red, white and blue bunting onto fences, porch rails and balconies.

- Place an American flag and a red, white and/or blue bow in any plant to instantly transform it into a holiday decoration.

- Decorate with blue denim (e.g., tablecloth) and complete the look with red and white stars of all sizes.

- Pull out your red, white and blue quilts to use as tablecloths and chair throws.

- Plant red and white geraniums in galvanized tin buckets.

From My Kitchen...and My Heart!

FLAG CAKE

1 recipe of your favorite white cake (mix or from scratch, your choice)

2 pts. fresh strawberries

1 pt. fresh blueberries

8 oz. Cool Whip (thawed), mixed with 1 3-oz. pkg. vanilla pudding; or white frosting

Bake your favorite cake recipe or mix in a 13 x 9 x 2-inch cake pan. Let cool.

Stem and cut the strawberries into halves, set aside on paper towels. Drain blueberries on paper towels.

Spread Cool Whip (or frosting) generously over the cake while in the pan.

In the top left-hand corner of the frosted cake, arrange the blueberries into an outline of a rectangle that is 5 inches wide and 4 inches tall. Press the berries down into the frosting.

Fill the blueberry outline in with the remaining blueberries. The blueberries will look best if placed in rows (the icing between them will resemble stars).

Place strawberry halves cut-side down in rows going across the cake horizontally, pressing them into the icing. The bottom stripe of the flag is red, so start the first row at the bottom.

Refrigerate until ready to serve.

TIP: Place strawberries and blueberries on top just before serving to prevent them from bleeding onto the icing.

· Halloween ·

October 31 always promises a night of fun. After all, what other holiday requires a costume? Halloween is: carved pumpkins, jack-o'-lanterns, skeletons and witches hats. Colors: black and orange. (Tip: Consider a black-and-white color scheme for a ghostly effect.)

PICTURE THIS...

- Make your own pumpkin patch. Complete with pumpkins, straw and scarecrows, it will easily carry over to Thanksgiving.

- Replace your front porch lighting with low wattage orange- or blue-tinted bulbs to set a foreboding stage for trick-or-treaters.

- Add cobwebs (available at most party stores) in your front lawn bushes, use them in choice corners of your home and selectively place miniature spiders in each web.

- Cover your furniture with white sheets to simulate a deserted haunted house.

- Scatter shrunken apple heads around your house for a spooky effect. Note: Start the process of drying them early as it takes a couple of weeks to reach perfection.

- Carve green peppers as jack-o-lanterns. You can have a whole row of them, and there are yellow, red and orange peppers to try as well.

- Arrange artificial sunflowers in a black wrought iron wheelbarrow for the designer's touch.

MARIANNE'S CASHEW BARS

Marianne, aunt

¼ lb. butter

1 c. graham crackers (crushed)

1 14-oz. can Eagle Brand sweetened condensed milk

1 6-oz. pkg. semi-sweet chocolate chips

1 c. flaked coconut

1 c. salted cashews (chopped)

Preheat oven to 325°.

In a 10 x 5-inch loaf pan, melt butter in oven. Sprinkle crumbs over butter; pour sweetened condensed milk evenly over crumbs.

Sprinkle with chips, then coconut and nuts; pressing down firmly.

Bake 35 minutes or until lightly browned.

Cool. Chill thoroughly, if desired.

Cut into bars. Store loosely covered at room temperature.

These bars are like potato chips. You can't eat just one!

· Birthday ·

The purpose of a birthday celebration is to make someone feel particularly special for an entire day. From having teddy bear picnics to offering pony rides and building forts in the yard, I've had them all (even birthday parties for the family dog). Birthdays are: presents, balloons, candles and wishes. Food: cake and ice cream.

PICTURE THIS...

- Decorate in the birthday boy or girl's (man or woman's) favorite colors with balloons, placemats, centerpieces, candles, sweets in candy jars, even doormats.

- Theme it (examples: baseball or wine tasting for adults; Batman or Barbie for children).

From My Kitchen...and My Heart!

COOKIE-FRUIT SALAD
....
Vonnie McMillin, mother

1 3-oz. pkg. vanilla instant pudding

1 c. milk

1 tsp. lemon juice

8-oz. Cool Whip, thawed

1 20-oz. can pineapple chunks, drained

1 15-oz. can fruit cocktail, drained

2 10½-oz. cans Mandarin oranges, drained

14-18 Keebler fudge striped cookies (crushed)

Beat together pudding, milk and lemon juice.

Lightly fold in Cool Whip, followed by the drained fruit—pineapple, fruit cocktail and oranges.

Mix crushed cookies into the salad, saving ½ of them to sprinkle on top.

Refrigerate until ready to serve.

BRING OUT THE BALLOONS!

OPPOSITE

Decorate your mantel for the celebration.

Anniversary

Light the candles, dim the lights and pull out your finest china to celebrate your wedding anniversary. Colors: black, white, metallics and jewel tones.

PICTURE THIS ...

- Go with traditional gift suggestions for the year of your celebration, e.g., 1st paper, 15th crystal, 25th silver and 50th gold.

- Decorate with framed photos of the couple at various stages of their marriage.

- Create a small replica of the couple's wedding cake to be used as the centerpiece.

- Think theme. If the couple married in Las Vegas, go with a casino theme; or if the duo loves to spend vacations at the shore, have a beach party.

- Most romantic idea: Have a bubble bath party, complete with scattered rose petals and a chilled bottle of champagne.

THE RIBBON CONNECTION

If you're decorating on a budget, the use of ribbons and bows will go a long way in adding elegance and charm without breaking the bank. Buy the ribbon when it's on sale and make your own bows. It's simple to do and simply elegant.

- Select ribbons in colors and patterns (consider plaids or florals) that coordinate with your decorating scheme. If you can't find anything that looks quite right, go with metallic silver, gold or my favorite—a black and white combo.

- Tie generous bows to chair backs, candlesticks, picks in plants, wreaths, garlands, basket handles, drapery tiebacks, stair railings and doorknobs.

- Choose a ribbon that you can untie and re-tie each year. This will save money in the long run, and you'll end up with a good collection.

- When the holidays are over, untie the ribbons and press them lightly. The bows won't get crushed and the ribbons will be ready to use for the next year.

- Use ribbons to decorate for all holidays.

SIX

No Rules-
Anything
Goes!

ecorate like no one is watching. I like things that create an unexpected surprise, items that are a bit off-kilter. In the world of design, my only hard-and-fast rule is there are no rules. Of course, there are guidelines, but some principles beg to be broken.

My philosophy is that the way to make a great statement is to go against the standard fare. But the key to its success is knowing how and where to break the rules.

Here's your assignment. Set aside the guidelines you've always heard and start fresh with what you like. Think outside the box. Try anything and everything to get the look you want. If you want to follow a trend, do so, but don't get too ahead of the game. On the other hand, don't follow trends—create your own.

CURRENT TRENDS

- Animal patterns (paired with hot pink or bright green)

- Polka dots

- Earthy colors

- The color chocolate—it's the new black

- Color combos: chocolate with red or green

- Avocado green—old color, new name (now called "wasabi")

- Popular colors of the 60s—psychedelic pink, retro purple and neon green

MIX AND DON'T MATCH

Operate by the hypothesis that opposites do attract.

How so? It can be as simple as using mismatched sets of china dishes or pairing dissimilar furniture shapes, e.g., a round table with a square nightstand.

Let's explore the potential of this theory's creativity with a single task: dining room chair selection. Your options are endless. Mix the chair styles using different designs of the same wood, similar styles in different woods or the exact same chairs (each painted a different color). Or pair vintage chairs with a contemporary chrome-and-glass table. In short, stray from the ordinary.

And stray from your house's interior. Extend this mix and don't match mantra to your patio. Paint old, iron chairs an assortment of colors; and use them around a distressed wooden table.

THE BLEND: OLD WITH NEW

When it comes to your décor, both modern and mature can exist harmoniously. This unlikely combo not only adds interest and character to your look, but also creates love for the history attached to an old treasure. My advice to achieving a good mix is to follow the 40-60 rule—40% old to 60% new—or visa versa. Either ratio works.

Even if you don't abide by the law of 40-60 (remember, no rule is rigid), never decorate a room with all old or all new pieces. If you're into a sleek style, incorporate a touch of old. Contemporary works well with a sprinkling of yesteryear because it adds warmth to this typically colder look. And don't forget, you can update anything old. If vintage leaves you cold, paint Grandpa's chair black (tip: black goes with any style) and upholster it with a modern fabric, such as brown leather or zebra print.

Paint old, iron chairs an assortment of colors...

$

RUMMAGE THROUGH
YOUR FAMILY'S
FORGOTTEN
KEEPSAKES FOR
DECORATIVE
TREASURES, SUCH
AS YOUR MOTHER'S
BEADED PURSES,
AND SHOWCASE
THE COLLECTION IN
A TEXTURED BASKET
ATOP YOUR VANITY.

$

The old/new equation can also apply to your kitchen. Consider this look: old wooden cabinets freshened with a new coat of paint and decorative hardware, vintage tile counters and state-of-the-art stainless appliances. Or it can be as simple as a flea market printer's cabinet used as an inventive wine holder.

MY HOUSE IS A MIXED COLLECTION OF OLD *AND* NEW

- The back hallway linen closet is a curio cupboard from a Texas farmhouse.

- My office table is a hand-me-down trunk.

- Collectible cupboards and new china cabinets blend to decorate my dining room.

- A high-end leopard skin chair in my living room is balanced by an antique rocker.

- The vintage dresser in my guest room holds the plasma television.

EXPECT THE UNEXPECTED

Think of common objects in uncommon ways. Utilize an item for a purpose other than its original intention. In my home, my mother's old game table serves as an end table. It fits perfectly. Had it not worked, there are solutions: repaint it, reconfigure it, rethink it.

THESE CREATIVE INNOVATIONS MAY SPARK IDEAS OF YOUR OWN:

- Use a seashell as a soap dish, a bud vase as a toothbrush holder, a covered candy dish for bath salts, maybe a silver toast rack to hold face cloths.

- In place of your family room curtain rod, use a tree branch of the same diameter for a rustic touch.

> BEWARE THAT SOME OLDER PIECES ARE SLIGHT IN SCALE AND MIGHT GET LOST WITH TODAY'S OVERSIZED FURNISHINGS.
> EXAMPLE:
> A TREASURED DESK TOO SMALL FOR MY HOME OFFICE WAS PLACED IN A NOOK OF MY KITCHEN.

- Stray from traditional wall art. Display an unexpected collection, such as an assembly of brightly painted window shutters.

- Go with a champagne holder to house a potted plant, rather than the traditional route.

- Create attractive shelving in a bathroom for your curio display by removing the door and painting the interior of your medicine cabinet.

- Place a candle on a bed of buttons at the bottom of a glass container.

- Consider a large ceramic vase in place of a standard umbrella stand.

- Substitute a treasured (but typically stored) quilt as your tablecloth.

- Use a heavy decorative bookend as a distinctive doorstop.

SCRUBBY SOLUTION

My own signature look is defined by furniture best described "scrubby." What exactly is this style? It's painted metal or wooden furniture that appears comfortably worn, almost as if delivered directly from your grandmother's house. Regardless of fact, scrubby furniture gives an appearance of history, of having a story to tell.

Whatever your scrubby selection—cupboard, hutch, side table, dining table, stool, chair, desk, headboard—it is a departure from the look of sameness. The purpose of a scrubby furniture piece can vary. It can be used to easily blend or to stand alone as the aah factor. Going the scrubby route is an inexpensive method to update heirlooms and a great way to use a piece you might otherwise discard. It adds the personal touch that says, "This house is mine."

$

LOOKING FOR A FAST, FRUGAL FIX FOR YOUR EXTRA ROOM? TRY THIS: SHOP AT A FLEA MARKET FOR THE ESSENTIALS— A HEADBOARD, SIDE TABLE AND CHAIR. SCRUB-ITIZE THEM. ADD NEW BED LINENS, A FUN QUILT AND DON'T FORGET TO LAYER. THEN FINISH THE LOOK WITH A COLORFUL THROW RUG AND VASE OF FRESH FLOWERS.

$

Scrub it into style

....

If you don't have an attic to scour for furniture that recalls the past, here's how to create your own heirloom-like pieces.

1. Find an iron or wooden chest, table, chair, desk or armoire, whatever you choose. Look for a basic selection or something distinctively different. Where to look? Thrift shops, garage sales and home (rummage through your for-the-Goodwill pile).

2. Decide on color—a single choice or a combination of two colors. When I've used two hues, I have selected from an assortment of pairings, including butter cream/sage, pink/white or black/red. Determine the dominate color and the underlying color. Example: a black chest of drawers with cherry red undertones.

3. Using the above example, paint two coats of the red "underlying" color. (Note: One paint coat does not give the desired depth of color.) Let each coat dry thoroughly. Now duplicate the process with the black "dominate" color.

4. Lightly sand the furniture where it would wear naturally (typically its edges), giving the appearance of a piece used lovingly. When working with two colors, sand through only the top color to reveal the second shade. If you've used one color, sand through the painted coat to the original surface.

5. The final step is the most fun. Add hardware to reflect your personality—distinctive hinges, drawer pulls and cabinet knobs.

If you consider this task out of your realm of expertise, seek a professional. It shouldn't be difficult to find a competent source. A substantial portion of my design business is aging and updating furniture.

> THE BUILT-IN WEAR OF SCRUBBY FURNITURE IS IDEAL FOR THE OUTDOORS, WHERE ITEMS WEATHER NATURALLY.

BRING ON THE FUNK!

Just say no to "boring." When you decorate, don't stop at normal. Be a bit of a rebel—pattern on pattern, texture on texture, pattern on texture, unexpected colors or "in" combos. Change it up.

Shorten a table by cutting its legs, substitute a door for a headboard or use a weathered wooden fence as a mantel top. Highlight your door or window with a wreath embellished by the unexpected, e.g., a kitchen wreath adorned with cooking utensils and a beautiful ribbon. Think unintended use, unexpected texture, unanticipated colors and unpredictable furniture arrangement.

Funky flair can even extend to your Christmas tree. Go with a wild color scheme, such as hot pink and lime green. Consider decorating with out-of-the-ordinary objects: your daughter's baby dolls, oversized numbers sparkling with glitter, even mismatched pieces of silverware hung by red velvet bows. And leopard ribbon always adds a fun touch.

BELOW:
Pattern on pattern for the indoors.
OPPOSITE:
Pattern on pattern for the outdoors.
OVERLEAF:
When you decorate, don't stop at normal.

$ TO UPDATE WITH A TRENDY HUE OR PATTERN, BUY PILLOWS IN THE "IN" COLOR OR PRINT—NOT A SOFA. IT IS A COST-CONSCIOUS SOLUTION TO STAYING IN STYLE. $

MORE IS MORE

I love *stuff*—all kinds of stuff—big stuff, small stuff, pretty stuff. So while it is not always wise to have more possessions, it's difficult to go wrong with thoughtful and tasteful details. These details can be as simple as beaded fringe on an accent pillow or as dominate as an architectural feature (French windows, circular staircase or wrought-iron railings).

More completes the look. It adds personality; it makes the difference. Interpreted literally, this is the style where you fill spaces, such as tabletops, wall space, floor space, shelves and exposed ledges. Open your cupboards and bring out your *stuff*. Use linens as throws, place big platters on top of your sideboard, have lead crystal bowls as catch-all trays. Fill these areas with lamps, mirrors, books, artwork, family photos, candles and florals. The result: cozy and cool!

This look isn't exclusive to the country style or the comfy cottage home. It's about measuring the amount of more to the look you seek. If you lean toward contemporary, for example, use three streamlined items to add personality.

The *more* mentality can be unsettling if you don't work within certain parameters: complementary colors, balance and the law of numbers.

THE RESULT OF TOO MANY FURNISHINGS IN A SPACE CAN BE OVERWHELMING, REPLICATING A CROWDED FURNITURE STORE RATHER THAN A COMFORTABLE ROOM.

COMPLEMENTARY COLORS: Work within a color scheme that reflects the style you seek, the mood you desire and the look you like. (Refer to *Chapter Four* for complete details.)

BALANCE: Keep items in scale with the room and with its other pieces. To accomplish this task: 1) vary the heights— high, medium, low; and 2) vary the sizes—large, medium and small.

NUMERICAL NOTION: Think in threes; if not, think in odd numbers. Three is the magic interior design number for balance and scale.

HARD AND FAST FACT

Though I encourage rule breaking, forever follow this regulation: decorate to create a comfortable, useable and livable home.

ABOVE:
Three is the magic number.

OPPOSITE:
Keep it balanced.

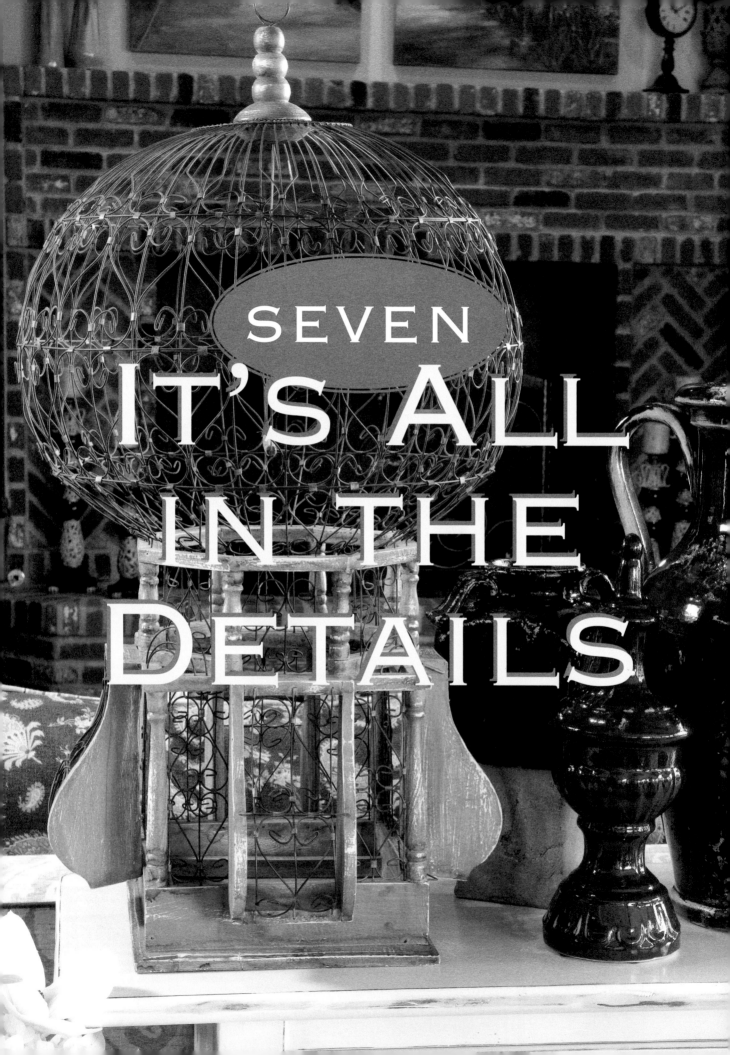

SEVEN

It's All in the Details

$\mathcal{L}$ ove is in the details" is a frequent Oprah Winfrey quote. Though I agree, my philosophy takes it one step further. Love is in the details, love is in your home.

It's no secret that attention to detail can transform a house from delightful to dazzling by highlighting architectural features or showcasing accessories. Thus, decorative details run the gamut, from the high mantel over your fireplace and eight-foot-tall doorways to your collection of mix-and-match dinnerware and a framed love letter from your father to your mother. While structural design might stretch your budget, the minimal expense (and effort) of accessorizing details may surprise you. For insight, read on.

ANALYZE HOW TO ACCESSORIZE

When you begin the process, the criteria for accessorizing success can be gauged by affirmative answers to a two-question test: 1) Do you love it? and; 2) Does it solve a design dilemma? To make the determination if an accessory falls into one of these categories, listen to your instincts.

Expand your shopping sites beyond department stores and interior design studios. Frequent art shows, craft fairs, antique shops, swap meets, even auctions. Cultivate a think-outside-the-box attitude when the subject is accessories.

Accents can affect the look of an entire room. But keep in mind that accessories do not work well side-by-side just because they're accessories. They succeed because of similar styles, similar looks and similar colors. And often, by just rearranging or re-adorning a room, you will feel as though you completely redecorated the space.

Your assignment: Begin with a small area of a single room. One of the hardest areas of the house to accessorize can be your kitchen counter, but not if you follow the above principles. And remember: When in doubt, keep it simple.

OPPOSITE
Cultivate a think-outside-the-box attitude when the subject is accessories.

OVERLEAF
Accessories succeed because of similar styles, similar looks and similar colors.

LIKE PAINTING BY NUMBERS

1. Ascribe to the law of sameness when arranging accessories. Think about it, even if the items aren't the same shape and color, a grouping of wooden hand mirrors on your powder room wall makes an appealing arrangement. Or assemble vintage sugar and creamer sets and showcase them atop an ornate silver tray. Why? The common theme. And remember: When it comes to collections, quantity is quality (resist the tendency to scatter a collection, piece by piece, around your house).

2. Achieve depth by staggering items displayed on a shelf. Forget straight lines and go for a look of interest, not inactivity.

3. Alter the altitude. Pairing accessories all of the same height can look bland. Vary the elevations by placing objects on books, platforms or small holders, if necessary.

4. Arrange your grouping around a single anchor if your first attempt falls flat. Never make the mistake of anointing two focal points. The result: Each would diminish the importance of the other, making neither special.

5. Accessorize with discrimination. To achieve this goal, edit the number of smaller pieces. Whether you seek to achieve subtle or high impact, the look of too many items is disconcerting.

ABOVE:
One of the hardest areas to accessorize
can be your kitchen counter.

ARRANGING
ACCESSORIES

SIMPLICITY OF SYMMETRY

Symmetrical style is a direct contradiction to the law of threes. Design's definition of symmetry is decorating in mirror images. And it looks best when working in an evenly balanced space, such as a pair of love seats flanking your fireplace. Symmetry can be achieved with the exact same accessories on either side of a common element or with objects that don't match perfectly but are approximately the same size, height or color.

Conversely, there's asymmetrical design, where the goal is not to create a double likeness. One of the easiest ways to illustrate symmetrical versus asymmetrical is to envision the different ways the top of a buffet can be decorated using basically the same items.

But whether your intention is to create a symmetrical or asymmetrical setting, use the following guideline to ensure success because balance is key (though in asymmetrical design, it is informal balance). Imagine you're using a scale. If either side of your composition tips the scale one way or the other, then you need to work on making things more visually equal.

LEFT:
Same buffet decorated symmetrically (above) and asymmetrically (below).

- Make it your own. Consider monograms on bed pillows, tablecloths, picture frames, etc. Choose a signature font, carrying it from room to room. In addition to your initials or your name, embroider a festive word or favorite sentiment on napkins. Numbers, such as your anniversary date, can be a 21st century twist to a monogram of initials.

- Fresh flowers versus artificial. Though fresh flowers are always the preference, don't despair if your budget or the time of year make it prohibitive. Go for artificial—but only artificial flowers that look genuine and are in the same colors as their real counterparts. The splurge will be worth it.

- Suspend an ornate but empty picture frame in front of your wall-mounted bathroom mirror to create the illusion of depth and for a dynamic flair. Or attach a fancy mirror to the door of your medicine cabinet to dress it up.

- Think like an architect and install out-of-sight strip lighting along the top or bottom of cabinets or within the recesses of your ceiling's molding. Or put a lamp on an automatic timer atop a cupboard for interesting lighting.

- Add creative detail to your slipcovers by mixing it up. Make them from an assortment of fabric remnants, using different print selections for the welting, pillows, arm rests and various sides of the seat cushions.

$

IF YOUR BUDGET DOESN'T ALLOW FOR REUPHOLSTERING, SPRING FOR A CUSTOM-MADE SLIPCOVER TO REINVENT A COUCH OR CHAIR.

$

$

Bring the outdoors into your home by painting a fanciful child-like scene on a window pane. Use water-soluble paint and you can easily illustrate every season, e.g., flowers in spring, perhaps a snowman during colder weather. If you have no artistic ability, fear not. The more elementary your painting, the more fun you'll have.

- Too many bedroom pillows? Never. My credo: Pile them on (round, square, oblong, neckroll and boudoir). Sure, your shams can match your comforter, but they don't have to.

- Hang a collection of family hats on the back of your bedroom door.

- Make a statement with a crystal chandelier hung above your bed, but pay attention to its scale.

- Don't neglect using your ceiling to showcase your creativity. Think of it as a canvas for overhead artistry. Or why not embellish your room by painting its beadboard ceiling an unexpected color?

- Use your windowsill to display a favorite collection, e.g., vases, seashells, paperweights, salt-and-pepper shakers, ceramic Limoges boxes, vintage glass bottles.

- Group all black-and-white or all color pictures together for wall displays and photo collections scattered about the house. Choose a basic theme for your frames; one that matches your overall style.

- To achieve a sophisticated library look, remove the jacket covers from your hardbound books and group them by color.

- Go green. Use plants to soften the look of any room.

- Always light the wick of a displayed candle (if only for a minute). If left perfectly untouched, it will look artificial.

- Give your room a finished appearance with decorative molding and trim. Don't forget your doors. Ornamental levers, knobs and pulls are cost-conscious embellishments.

- In a predominately white, beige or pastel setting, a brightly-painted furniture piece shouts "look at me." By virtue of color alone, it becomes important and your room's focal element.

- When something just doesn't work, paint it.

ROAD RULES

The purpose of rules is to give guidelines; but they can be broken to fit your needs if done so with thoughtful deliberation. Follow some of these rules, or don't. It's your call.

DOS—
TRY IT, YOU MIGHT LIKE IT

- Design to scale; the tendency is to buy furniture that is too small.

- Forgo formality with an asymmetrical floor plan.

- Bring a touch of nature into every room with items such as fresh flowers, greenery or seashells. Other examples: a pomegranate-filled wooden bowl or a glass vase piled with pinecones.

- Rather than hanging art on the wall above a table, sit it atop the table leaning casually against the wall.

  - Incorporate dressmaker touches, e.g., pintucks, appliqués and rusching, to get a custom look when having drapes, pillows and cushions sewn.

  - Play to the power of one. Example: Place a single stem of the same flower in each one of three identical glass vases running along the center of a table.

  - Consider the indoor use of garden furniture.

DON'TS—
RARELY WORKS; EXPERIMENT AT YOUR OWN RISK

- Place everything against walls. Rather, float some of your furniture and arrange pieces at angles to combat a room's stagnant style.

- Crowd a doorway with a large piece of furniture.

- Suspend a chandelier too far from the tabletop. The ideal height is approximately 28 inches above the table's surface (unless your centerpiece is extremely high).

- Hang pictures too high.

- Buy an assortment of small items, as opposed to a single, dramatic piece.

EIGHT

FRESHEN UP

*K*eeping your home fresh is like "year-round" spring cleaning. It's not limited to one season. The good news is that freshening your home (whatever time of year) doesn't have to be a complete re-do. An update can be as easy as new kitchen rugs, different doormats, a seasonal wreath and changing out everyday items, such as kitchenware and bed linens.

And remember, there is no need to use all of your accessories all of the time. Think of your adornments as a curator views pieces in a museum collection. Rotate them in and out of your home and from room to room. Easy examples include moving your sofa pillows into the bedroom or resurrecting the funky chest from the attic for your living room. In my own home, I circulate my treasured rocking chairs throughout the house—from my kitchen sitting area to the head of the dining room table to the family room next to the fireplace. Bottom line: Small changes can be significant.

COZY UP TO THE CALENDAR

Pay attention to the season and decorate to reflect it. Here are some of my favorite fast fixes:

FAST FIX 1: Slipcover your furniture. Nothing ushers in spring better than voile dining room chair covers; winter arrives when you slipcover your couch in velvet.

FAST FIX 2: Fill your summer fireplace with flowers or candles or place a screen with a garden scene in front of the fireplace.

FAST FIX 3: Strategically place accessories and potted plants on your stairway to shout the season.

FAST FIX 4: Revitalize a room with a wild patterned rug or a colored one reflective of the season.

FAST FIX 5: Hang a decorative curtain to camouflage your home's utility area when it's not in use.

FAST FIX 6: Take inspiration from the outdoors. Bring nature inside with a fresh garland in your winter cabin or a bleached driftwood doorstop at your beach retreat.

FAST FIX 7: Be creative with an eyesore; paint a seasonal mural on a utilitarian storage shed.

TOP ROW:
Hang a decorative curtain to camouflage your home's utlity area.

BOTTOM:
Paint a seasonal mural on a utilitarian storage shed.

OPPOSITE:
Place accessories and potted plants on your stairway to shout the season.

ABOVE:
Reposition your furniture for the seasons.

BELOW:
Place furniture at unexpected angles.

FURNITURE "FRESH"

Freshening a room may not require a single purchase when you rearrange, not redecorate. Just follow these tips of the trade when your look becomes stale.

- Reposition the furniture. During cold weather, place your couch and chairs closer to the fireplace to enjoy its warmth and to create a cozy place to read and chat. In warmer months, rearrange your furniture so the seating faces outward to the view.

- Create clusters.

- Pare down. Simplify your life along with the look.

- Place furniture at unexpected angles.

- For an eternally fresh look, rearrange the furniture several times a year.

SCENT SENSE

Use the sense of smell to make your home feel loved. You can constantly set different, inviting moods. It's as obvious as newly-cut flowers, freshly-baked cookies, lit candles and potpourri, and as simple as open windows and gaping doors.

Acknowledge that scents change with the season. Match them to the time of the year.

Spring
gardenia, lavender, violet

Summer
grapefruit, sandalwood, verbena

Fall
cranberry, pumpkin, spiced orange, cinnamon

Winter
evergreen, peppermint, vanilla

COLOR IT FRESH

Color is an inexpensive but effective way to brighten your home, though it is one of the most frightening changes to a novice decorator. No problem: The remedy for a poor color choice is as easy as a fresh can of paint and a free afternoon.

1. Use color to immerse into the season. Example: fall/winter—brown, orange, red, burgundy, hunter green; spring/summer—green, pink, blue, white, yellow. And don't forget to accessorize to complete the look.

2. To further brighten a newly colored wall, paint the molding white.

3. Unify mismatched wooden furniture pieces with a fresh coat of the same paint color and the same colorful upholstery fabric.

4. To change a room's look, introduce one prominent new color through accessories—such as pillows, flowers, throws or artwork.

Use a splash of color to add personality, whether it's bright red knobs on Grandma's wooden dresser, hot pink checkered pillows in the guest room or big, black bows to accent the backs of your dining room chairs.

LEFT AND RIGHT: Use color to immerse into the season. Example: fall/winter—brown, orange, red, burgundy, hunter green; spring/summer—green, pink, blue, white, yellow.

$

EXTEND YOUR MINI-MAKEOVER
TO YOUR HOME'S EXTERIOR.
IT'S AS SIMPLE AS REPAINTING
THE TRIM AND FRONT DOOR
OF YOUR HOUSE, REPLACING
OVERGROWN SHRUBS AND
ADDING PIECES OF OUTDOOR
FURNITURE. AND WHEN
THE SEASON PERMITS, BRING
IN A TOUCH OF COLOR WITH
FLOWERS.

$

NINE

Your Final Room: The Outdoors

*F*inished? Not so fast. You may think your home decorating project is complete, but it is not until your attention has focused out of doors.

There are no complicated designer tricks to fresh-air style, just common sense tips.

- Outdoor space should flow easily to and from the rooms of your house and coordinate with the exterior *and* interior of your home.

- Your outdoor advantage is that Mother Nature has provided you a glorious color scheme. If you follow this pre-ordained palette, you can never go wrong.

- Decorate your outdoor space with indoor comforts, but make it functional. Use soft cushions and pillows with chairs and ottomans, and scatter small tables throughout. Synthetic wicker and rattan furniture, coupled with weather-resistant outdoor fabrics (which today can be damasks, silks, velvets and look-alike leathers) make any look possible.

- Keep your exterior fresh. Don't let your fabrics fade or the plants die. Protect your furniture with clear plastic when not in use to keep it clean.

- Strive for versatility, making the transition from a daylight playground to an evening-and-entertainment getaway an easy one. Select furniture that can be effortlessly arranged to accommodate assorted seating needs (e.g., stacking chairs, folding tables and easily stored floor cushions).

LAT

NOT ONLY ARE TODAY'S OUTDOOR TEXTILES WATER, STAIN, FADE AND MILDEW RESISTANT, BUT THEIR COLORS AND PRINTS ARE AS VIVID AS THEIR INDOOR COUNTERPARTS. CONSIDER FABRIC SELECTIONS THAT ARE EXTENSIONS OF YOUR INTERIOR CHOICES.

PORCH PERFECTION

Houses with front porches have made a comeback. In the late 1800s to mid-1900s, houses were built with a front porch to allow the family to visit with one another, greet passersby and simply sit.

So I replicated the past in my home— a front porch with loungers, gliders and a row of rocking chairs—a yesteryear's porch perfect for eating sugar cookies and sipping iced tea with mint and lemon.

Keep your entrance fresh. It is important that when visitors approach your home, they see that you love it and they know that you care. Make it pretty with a door wreath, potted plants, fresh paint and anything inviting.

PATIO PREVIEW

Your patio is an extension of your house. It's your outdoor family room. Design it to be as important as your home's other rooms, comfy and inviting where people want to come and sit. Create a retreat from the interior of your home, giving it the feel that you're on vacation. The key is to design a patio according to your plans for using it.

You have unlimited options. Include a fire element (candles, year-round white Christmas lights, lanterns, tiki torches or fire pit). Use a water element (water fountain, pond with koi or a pool). And there are additional enhancements: gazebo, palapa, a poolside cabana, a simple Buddha or music playing sounds from nature in the background. A premium patio might include an outdoor kitchen (complete with a blender for mixing

LA

$

FOR A COSMOPOLITAN FLAIR TO A COVERED PORCH, HANG DRAPERIES THAT FOLD BACK GRACEFULLY (IF MONEY IS AN ISSUE, SUBSTITUTE COLORFUL SHEETS FOR THE FABRIC).

$

margaritas), a plasma television and a wood-burning brick oven (for roasting pizzas, meats and breads). But it's all about you. What do you want? What do you like to do?

Don't forget to maintain a relationship between nature and your patio. My own patio has a cage for our pet canary, Tweetie, who wakes us each morning with singing. And I added a small water fountain as the sound of water is always soothing. The result is that we are frequently outdoors because we've created an atmosphere of serenity.

Keep in mind that none of the above is necessary, though all of the above are possibilities toward designing your perfect patio.

SET UP YOUR PLAY AREA SO THAT YOU CAN SEE IT. ATTRACT THE KIDS
WITH BRIGHT COLORS, PLASTICWARE, FLOATIES, GAMES AND FUN, E.G., TETHER-
BALL, TRAMPOLINE, HORSESHOES, HOPSCOTCH, BADMINTON, PLAY DOUGH,
BOTTLES OF BUBBLES AND BUCKETS OF CHALK. MAKE IT PRACTICAL AND SAFE.
EXAMPLE: DON'T PLACE THE BASKETBALL COURT NEXT TO THE SWIMMING POOL.

GARDEN DELIGHTS

Because it can readily satisfy your craving for fresh air and sunshine, gardening is an important outlet for those of us harried by this busy world. Its produce—spring flowers and summer vegetables—makes it practical and all the more rewarding.

Use a mix of reproduction and vintage items to make your garden another thoughtful addition to your home. Visit gardening stores and antique shops in search of birdbaths, urns, metal gates, wooden benches, colorful pottery and yard art. And seek out your mother's old gardening tools and watering cans.

Weather-worn pieces from the garden take on additional charm when mixed with floral fabrics, botanical prints and crisp colors. Again, pair the old with the new. It works.

HERE'S THE DIRT ON GARDENS

Though there are many styles of gardens, the old fashioned cottage garden is my all-time favorite. It is a casual, informal collection of flowering plants and its style gives the freedom to be untamed or restrained, whatever look you seek.

The cottage-style garden is a mix of perennials, shrub roses and annuals all fusing into one another as they mature, looking as if seeded by nature. Remember: A true cottage garden must have roses.

$

YOU CAN MAKE YOUR OWN YARD ART BY PLACING ANYTHING ON A STICK, E.G., A PUMPKIN, BIRDHOUSE, GARDEN TOOL, EVEN AN OLD HOUSEHOLD ITEM. AND USE ANYTHING AS YOUR STICK—MAYBE A GARDEN RAKE.

GROW A VEGETABLE GARDEN, PLANTING WHAT YOU EAT AND COOK. MARK YOUR VEGETABLES WITH YARD ART. MAKE IT A FAMILY AFFAIR BY GETTING THE KIDS INVOLVED.

LITTLE THINGS COUNT

A decorative touch in my own backyard is
an antique iron bed frame set in soil with
my strawberry patch planted inside.

FAR LEFT:
Use your yard to display collections.

LEFT:
Plant an herbal garden inside a hand-
painted wooden chest.

Group your plants by their water, food and sun requirements
and give them space to grow to adult size. Fill in the holes with
annuals, short-lived perennials and container plants. Place the
garden where it can be enjoyed daily (example: in view of your
kitchen's picture window).

- Make a statement with herbs. It can be as simple as individually potted plants or as extensive as an herbal garden planted inside a hand-painted wooden chest.

- Add color to your lawn by planting an assortment of annuals at the base of your trees, changing them with the seasons.

- Consider conventional color combinations, such as red and white, for porch furniture. And when needed, give your wicker furniture and rocking chairs a renewed look with a fresh coat of paint (good choices: white, green, brown or black).

- Think of your yard as another place to display collections, perhaps a grouping of birdhouses.

- Go with a decorative trellis and accent it with seasonal flowers in different colors.

OUTDOOR ENTERTAINMENT CENTER

Enjoying the outdoors can be as simple as including a white picnic table or having sterno logs in a clay chimenea; anything to give you a reason to be outside. Add a place to cook and provide for comfortable temperature (winter—heaters; summer—shade). But don't forget a small getaway area for relaxation.

$

NO WORRIES IF YOUR BACKYARD IS TOO SMALL FOR A TRADITIONAL GARDEN. BRING THE JOY OF NATURE AND FLOWERS ONTO YOUR PATIO WITH HANGING BASKETS OR PLANTED BOXES PEEKING INTO YOUR WINDOWS.

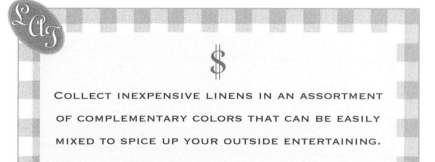

$

COLLECT INEXPENSIVE LINENS IN AN ASSORTMENT OF COMPLEMENTARY COLORS THAT CAN BE EASILY MIXED TO SPICE UP YOUR OUTSIDE ENTERTAINING.

How to Throw a Party...
Any Party

The charm of an al fresco meal can be its casual style: potted plants, quilted tablecloths, just-picked vegetables and freshly made sandwiches wrapped like gifts in brown kraft paper and tied with ribbon bows. But outdoors does not strictly dictate informality, for a fresh-air get together can be as fancy as you desire. However, fancy or not, every party requires a little forethought.

First, the Theme

Select a color, a cuisine or go with the season (if summer had an official fabric, it would be red gingham). Should you desire the crisp sophisticated look of white, pair your white linens with a centerpiece of white roses or tulips and accent with white tea lights. A five-course dinner and a bubbly glass of champagne will complete the party. Or set the tone of a fiesta with the bright color scheme found in a Mexican blanket, e.g., red tablecloth, green napkins, yellow placemats and a cactus centerpiece.

Second, the Accessories

To decorate your table, open your closets and use your imagination. Scour your home for accessories that work with your theme. Example: A pasta-and-wine evening can be complemented by your red and green plaid tablecloth, wicker baskets brimming with Italian bread loaves and decorative bottles of olive oil.

Third, the Table

For visual interest, vary the heights of your displayed food on the serving table. Place each dish at a different elevation atop items such as a cake stand, upside down salad bowl or ice bucket. Cover your makeshift stands with cloth napkins and make sure your platters are secure.

My Thoughts, Your Home

Remember, your home is a snapshot of the family who lives in it.

The wisest template for decorating is your imagination. My best advice is to live vicariously through no one. Learn to edit your 'to-do' list down to your 'really want to-do' list. Avoid trend chasing and master sorting through seasonal hype to spice up your space. You'll know when the chemistry clicks.

So break out your creativity, be resourceful and, when in doubt, seek the help of a professional to pull it all together. But however you do it, be mindful that decorating is not an assignment, it's an attitude.

To your success!

Letter of Love

At Home With Laurie Ann was written from my many years of living and decorating. Decorating is my passion, my friend, my favorite pastime. Every suggestion shared with you in this book is one that I have personally tried and thoroughly enjoyed.

Believe me, there are no boundaries in design. What matters is that you love your home. And it matters how you feel when you are at home. Decorate toward these goals, and create a home that reflects your heartfelt intentions.

Life is precious. So, make it prettier, more comfortable and more important. Now go and rejoice in your projects, your parties and your home. As Mary Engelbreit suggests, "Bloom where you're planted."

I love home, and I live to help people decorate homes they love. Enjoy this book, enjoy the adventure.

Happy decorating and God bless,

Laurie Ann McDonald Ray

GLOSSARY

Accent colors: Contrasting colors used to enliven room schemes.

Ambient lighting: Provides an overall wash of light.

Analogous colors: Any series of colors adjacent on the color wheel.

Antique: An object 100 or more years old.

Antiquing: A technique for applying paint, varnish or glaze to a surface; then blotting it to suggest age.

Appliqué: A decoration made by cutting pieces of one material and applying them to the surface of another.

Asymmetrical: An arrangement that lacks similarity in size, shape and relative position of its corresponding parts.

Balance: A state of equilibrium; can be symmetrical or asymmetrical.

Beadboard: Vertical wood paneling; its origins can be traced to 19th Victorian and cottage-style homes.

Built-in: An element such as a bookcase or cabinetry that is built into a wall or an existing frame.

Chair rail: A molding, usually of wood, running along a wall at the height of chair backs.

Chintz: Printed cotton, often glazed.

Color wheel: A pie-shaped diagram showing the relationship of primary colors and the secondary colors produced as a result of their combination.

Complementary colors: Colors that are opposite each other on the color wheel.

Cornice: Horizontal molding at the top of a wall.

Decoupage: Cutouts of paper or other materials applied to various surfaces, then varnished for permanence.

Dimmer switch: A type of light switch that allows light levels to be controlled at various gradations, from dim to bright.

Downlight: A spotlight that casts light downward, which is recessed or attached to the ceiling.

Drop-leaf table: A table with hinged leaves that can be folded down.

Faux: French for "false;" a term to describe something that is simulated.

Flat finish: A non-reflective finish.

Glazing: A decorative paint technique whereby a film of color is applied to a painted surface to create a semi-transparent effect.

Gloss: A type of paint that dries to a high sheen.

Grass cloth: A type of wall covering made of woven reeds and dried grasses.

Hardware: Exterior knobs, handles and trim used on furniture; the material is typically wood, plastic or metal-plated.

Harmony: A consistent, orderly or pleasing arrangement of parts.

Holdbacks: Brackets (usually decorative) that mount to either side of a window to hold back the draperies.

Hue: The name of a color, such as red, blue or yellow.

Incandescent light: The kind of light that is produced by standard light bulbs.

Indirect light: A more subdued type of lighting that is reflected from a surface, such as a wall or ceiling.

Lacquer: A hard varnish that is applied in many layers then polished to a high sheen.

Marbling: A decorative paint technique used to create the look of real marble.

Matte: A flat paint finish with no shine or luster.

Modular furniture: Seating or storage units designed to fit many configurations.

Monochromatic scheme: A color scheme limited to one color in various tones.

Occasional furniture: Small items such as coffee tables, lamp tables or tea carts that are used as accent pieces. (eliminate comma "lamp tables or tea carts")

Palette: Term used to describe a range of colors, as in the color scheme of a room.

Parquet: Inlaid geometric patterns of wood; used primarily in flooring.

Picture rail: A molding placed high on a wall as a means for suspending artwork.

Primary colors: Red, blue and yellow (from which all colors are derived); they cannot be produced by mixing other colors.

Proportion: Aesthetic arrangement of parts considered in relation to the whole; in terms of size, quantity, number and ratio.

Recessed downlights: Lighting built into the ceiling that casts light downward.

Reproduction: An exact, or nearly exact, copy of an original design.

Satin: A soft sheen finish.

Scale: A term referring to the size of objects in relation to each other and the human body; in decorating, good scale is the result of an eye-pleasing relationship between furnishings, other objects and the space in which they are used.

Sconce: A space saving, wall-mounted lighting fixture that can cast light upwards, downwards or sideways.

Scrubby: Painted or metal furniture that shows wear and appears old.

Secondary colors: Colors reproduced by mixing two primary colors (example: forming the color green by combining yellow and blue).

Shade: The darker values of a particular color obtained by mixing the color with black.

Slipcovers: Removable fabric covers for upholstered furniture.

Sponging: A paint technique involving the layer by layer application of opaque and translucent paint colors with a sponge.

Symmetrical: Having similarity in size, shape and relative position of corresponding parts.

Task lighting: Location specific lighting, like a lamp for reading or a fixture over a game table.

Tieback: A fastener attached to the sides of a window to hold back curtains.

Tint: The lighter values of a particular color obtained by mixing the color with white.

Tone: The darkness or lightness of a color; different colors may be of the same tone.

Track lighting: Individual sources of lighting mounted on a track that can be aimed to highlight architectural details and favorite objects.

Trompe l'oeil: French for "fool the eye;" a two-dimensional painting designed to look three-dimensional.

Tumbled marble tile: Tile that lends itself to a more distressed, old-fashioned and rustic look.

Uplight: A fixture that directs light toward the ceiling.

Valance: A drapery treatment made of fabric or wood used as a heading.

Value: A term describing the lightness (tints) or darkness (shades) of a color.

Wainscoting: Wood paneling applied to walls from baseboards to a desired height below the chair rail.

Welt: A cord along the seam or border edge of a pillow, cushion or upholstered furniture.

INDEX